Steward's Close Meadow

52

Higden's Close 115

174

113

The Little Paddock 91

93 Long's Hill

Steward's Close

60

67 66 65 64 63 62 61 60 59 58 57 56 55 54

Close

48 49 51

47

50 shepherds post

Sheep Martin's Field

house Close

Causeyhead

108

Bann Lands

111

Follery Close

110 Lower Bishop's Close

70 Biddle's Field

109 Upper Bishop's Close

King of Prussia

Green Hill

107 Lane's Lower Ground

The Bymel Close

124

108

109
9. 2. 20

7.

86 First Mearse

87 Second Mearse

88 Third Mearse

Fourth

85 Old Abbey Orchard

96 Robert's Mearse

92 Seventh Mearse

7.1.5?

128

112

95

Lower Kingate

93 Upper Kingate

Sixt

97 Lower Paddock

90 Upper Paddock

The

YESTERDAY'S TOWN: EVESHAM

View from Waterside c 1865

Sketches of Evesham.

YESTERDAY'S TOWN:
EVESHAM

A BRIEF ACCOUNT OF THE TOWN
FROM c.1840-1940

BY
BENJAMIN G. COX
AND
D. GORDON ALCOCK

BARRACUDA BOOKS LIMITED
BUCKINGHAM ENGLAND
MCMLXXIX

PUBLISHED BY BARRACUDA BOOKS LIMITED
BUCKINGHAM, ENGLAND
AND PRINTED BY
BOWMAN-ROCASTLE LIMITED
HERTFORD, ENGLAND

BOUND BY
BOOKBINDERS OF LONDON LIMITED
LONDON N5

JACKET PRINTED BY
WHITE CRESCENT PRESS LIMITED
LUTON, ENGLAND

LITHOGRAPHY BY
SOUTH MIDLANDS LITHOPLATES LIMITED
LUTON, ENGLAND

TEXT SET IN 11pt PRESS ROMAN
BY BUSIPRINT LIMITED
BUCKINGHAM, ENGLAND

DISPLAY TYPE SET
BY SOUTH BUCKS TYPESETTERS LIMITED
BEACONSFIELD, ENGLAND

ISBN 0 86023 105 4

CONTENTS

INTRODUCTION

One of the recurring themes in any conversation about Evesham's past is the town's good fortune in the comparative lack of change in its appearance. So many towns have suffered developers' blight since the forties that Evesham stands out as one of the few to retain so much of its heritage. It was perhaps this, together with the renewed interest of modern times in the community's past, that gave the impetus to Ben Cox's *Book of Evesham* when it appeared in 1977, so that it went into a second impression within a year. The town's welcome for that brief but comprehensive view of its past focussed attention on the wealth of other material within the Evesham Historical Society's archives that, of necessity, was excluded from that volume. In particular, much of value and interest exists for the period 1840-1940 which, if included, would have unbalanced a record that spanned prehistory to modern times. The question immediately arose: what was to become of this unused material?

Evesham is fortunate in possessing a fine Museum, much of its excellence due to the personal enthusiasm, dedication and expertise of Ben Cox as founder member, Vice-President and Chairman of the Society, and Honorary Curator, and of Gordon Alcock as resident custodian. Both were well placed to attempt an answer to the question, and the final motivation was supplied when Evesham bookseller David Eaves suggested that an informed picture book for the period would ideally supplement the previous volume. This proposal immediately fell into place, for as publishers of *The Book of Evesham,* we had already faced similar considerations in Worcester and our own original hometown of Chesham, and had evolved an appropriate formula which we called *Yesterday's Town*.

Gordon Alcock tackled the illustrations, drawing on the vast body of material in his care. This has involved him in many hours of tedious work in the dark-room turning originals of variable quality into reproducible photographs, and his attention to detail and eye for atmosphere is evident in every page of pictures in this delightful book. The final selection was winnowed out from over 600 originals, none of which have appeared in any other publication. Of necessity, even now many pictures remain unused, and still more have come into the Society's hands since work began. Nonetheless, those that are included provide an accurate and fascinating reflection of the period.

Throughout the months of preparation, Ben Cox involved himself directly in the process of selection, parallelling this with an extension of his original, intensive research into the town's past, to provide a text commentary which brings back to life the people, places and events of Evesham's 19th and early 20th century heritage in some detail, yet with an affectionate concern for both the significant and the curious.

For many this book will provide a nostalgic journey; for others it will be a source of factual interest. We hope it will inform and entertain all who read it, supplement *The Book of Evesham* for those who have it, lead many to a greater interest in the town's past, will instruct younger readers without boring them, and above all, serve as a pleasant reflection of one of England's most pleasant small towns.

TO THE WORSHIPFUL THE

Mayor of Evesham.

SIR,

WE THE UNDERSIGNED, Burgesses and Inhabitants of the BOROUGH OF EVESHAM, and its Vicinity, most respectfully request you to summon a PUBLIC MEETING, to take the necessary steps for the purpose of presenting a Loyal and dutiful Address to the Queen, expressive of congratulation upon Her Majesty's accession to the Throne of her Ancestors, and of sincere condolence for the heavy affliction with which it has pleased Almighty Providence to visit Her Majesty and these Realms: and that at such Meeting there may be taken into consideration the propriety of presenting an Address of condolence and sympathy in the bereavement of Her Majesty the Queen Dowager.

Evesham, July 26th, 1837.

G. RUSHOUT	W. A. BYRCH
P. BORTHWICK	J. R. GRIFFITHS
THO. BLAYNEY	B. MURRELL
ROBERT BLAYNEY	J. R. AMHERST
REV. J. MARSHALL	HENRY BROWN
WM. SOLEY	WM. PULLIN
JOSEPH HARLING	WM. BARNES
WM. BYRCH	HENRY HIRON
DANIEL BAZALGETTE	JOHN BONAKER
ALFRED CAMPBELL COOPER	NATHAN IZOD

Bengeworth, 26 July, 1837.

In consequence of the above requisition, and for the Loyal & Constitutional purposes thereof, I do hereby convene a Meeting of the Burgesses and Inhabitants of the Borough of Evesham and its Vicinity, to be holden at the TOWN-HALL, in the said Borough, at the hour of Eleven in the Forenoon, on FRIDAY the 28th day of July instant.

Thomas Beale Cooper,
MAYOR.

Printed by J. PEARCE, Bridge-Street, Evesham.

Notice of 1837 loyal address.

ODD FELLOWS BALL,

Will take place at

THE TOWN-HALL, EVESHAM,

On FRIDAY, JANUARY 20th, 1843,

FOR THE BENEFIT OF THE

WIDOWS' & ORPHANS' INSTITUTION,

When the favour of your company, and that of your
friends, will be esteemed.

As the above Institution is for no less an object than that of
clothing, educating, and relieving the wants of the Orphans, Children, and Widows of departed Brothers of the Order, and to give
to the Widow and Fatherless the cheering and delightful assurance
that some aid is in store to succour and relieve them if in distress,
the Committee trust that a generous public will act in co-operation
and support to carry out so laudable an object.

Stewards:

T. F. SMITH, Esq.	THOMAS WHITE, Esq.
T. SARGANT, Esq.	JOHN NEW, Esq.
JOHN BONAKER, Esq.	J. B. HAYNES, Esq.
THOS. N. FOSTER, Esq.	OSWALD CHEEK, Esq.
Mr. GEORGE AGG	Mr. T. NEW
Mr. Z. HUGHES	Mr. W. W. HALL
Mr. FRANCIS HILL	Mr JOHN W. PHILLIPS
Mr. J. WOODWARD	Mr. JAMES GROVE
Mr. E. HAYNES	Mr. EDWARD MORGAN
Mr. W. ARTON	Mr. GEORGE TOVEY

DANCING TO COMMENCE AT EIGHT O'CLOCK.

*Tickets, including Refreshments, 2s. 6d. each, to be had at the
Lamb, and Rose & Crown Inns.*

January 12th, 1843.   ⌊Pearce, Pr.

Notice of Oddfellows ball 1843.

[George May, Albion Press, Evesham.]

No.   22 Sept 1820

Messrs. Oldaker, Day, Lavender, & Murrell,

BANKERS, EVESHAM.

Pay   *Self*   *or Bearer*

One Pound 19/2 on a/c
of Bills as on the other side.

£1-19-2   J. Atkins

No.   3rd June 1842

To the Gloucestershire Banking Company,

at the Bank, EVESHAM.

Pay to Edwd Gillam White or Bearer
Thirty five pounds
Ja Evesham Commrs

£ 35   X

Early Evesham bankers' cheques,
(Andrew Watton collection).

NOTICE.

All Persons are requested not to use any Nets for the catching or taking of FISH ; nor any Engines, Poachings, Traps, Trimmers, nor Lines for the catching or taking of EELS in the River Avon, from Evesham Bridge, up to Offenham Bridge, now Offenham Boat. I WILLIAM BARNES, now Rent the said Fishery, and intend to protect it for the benefit of Anglers.

Therefore any Person or Persons trespassing after this Public Notice, will be prosecuted according to Law.

WILLIAM BARNES.

Evesham, March 20th, 1849.

J. Pearce, Printer, Evesham.

Fishing rights notice, 1849.

AT A PUBLIC MEETING

AT THE

TOWN-HALL, EVESHAM,

ON THE 1st OF DECEMBER, 1851,

FOR THE PURPOSE OF MAKING

RULES & REGULATIONS

FOR THE HOLDING OF

THE CORN MARKET

THEREIN,

B. WORKMAN, ESQ.

HAVING BEEN APPOINTED CHAIRMAN,

It was Resolved that the thanks of this Meeting be given to the Mayor and Council of the Borough for their ready acquiescence to our Requisition for the use of the said Town Hall; and that the Conditions expressed in their Order relating thereto be adopted; and that the Corn Market Committee, to be this day appointed, or any three or more of them, shall be empowered by and on the behalf of the Frequenters of the said Market to enter into an Agreement with the said Council, conformably to the Conditions above alluded to, and to the tenor or effect following:—Namely, to pay the annual Rent of £10 for the use of the said Hall, in equal portions half-yearly, to the Treasurer of the Borough Fund; (which sum the said Council have calculated will be expended by them in the cleaning, painting, and repairing the damage to be done to the said Hall, exclusive of breakage of windows.)

To agree that the said Rent shall commence as and from the 1st day of January next, and that the holding shall be considered as a letting from year to year; to cease upon either party giving three calendar months' notice previous to the 1st day of January in any one year of an intention to determine the same.

And, conformably to the said Conditions, It has been Resolved that the said Town Hall shall be opened for the purposes of a Corn Market upon every Monday (not being a Fair-day) at ten minutes before Two o'clock, and closed again at a quarter-past Four o'clock; and shall be opened upon every Fair-day at One o'clock, and closed at Four o'clock in the Afternoon. And that the first time of such opening shall be at One o'clock on MONDAY next the 8th of DECEMBER, being a Fair-day.

Further, that the said Town Hall shall be wholly devoted during the hours above mentioned to the general purposes of a Corn Market, but wherein no Corn or other Articles in bulk shall be pitched for Sale.

And it has been this day further Resolved, that an Entrance-fee of 3d. shall be taken of every person entering the Hall upon every Monday and Fair-day, during the hours of market business: but that a pre-payment of 10s. 6d. shall free each payor from further fees up to the end of the year 1852; and every such pre-payment at the commencement of every following year shall free him during the whole of the same year.

That each Person requiring a Stand shall pay in advance the annual sum of £1 1s. 0d. for the use thereof; but which payment will be taken in lieu of other Entrance-fee from such Payor.

That the following Gentlemen are hereby appointed

" The Evesham Corn Market Committee."—viz.

THE MAYOR OF THE BOROUGH FOR THE TIME BEING.

Mr. JAMES ASHWIN,	Mr. JOHN COLLINS,
Mr. B. WORKMAN,	Mr. JOSEPH SMITH,
Mr. T. N. FOSTER,	Mr. NATHAN IZOD,
Mr. JOHN GOODWIN,	Mr. JOHN MARSHALL,
Mr. BENJAMIN BOMFORD, Jun.	HARVINGTON,
Mr. JOHN PITTS,	Mr. WILLIAM BARNES,

(three of whom to be a quorum) who are empowered by this Meeting to make such orders (not being provided) as they may think proper, for the Management of the said Market and the Collection of Fees and Subscriptions. That their period of office will be determined upon the first Monday in January, 1853; but every or any member of the present Committee may be re-appointed for that or any subsequent year.

That Mr. HENRY HIRON is appointed Treasurer, and Mr. JOHN SAUNDERS Honorary Secretary to the said Committee.

That (pursuant to a requirement of the said Council) on no pretence whatever shall the Committee or any Person be permitted to drive any Nails into the Walls, Wainscot, or Floors of the said Hall, or do any wilful damage therein.

And, according with the desire of the said Mayor and Council, (in whom the holding and keeping the said Market is vested by Charter) it is reasonably expected that no attempt will be made to continue to hold the Corn Market within the Street as heretofore to the obstruction of the Public Thoroughfare, and in a place so liable to personal Injury and Inconvenience, and therefore

It has been this day Resolved, to call in aid the Authority of the Council to prevent the same, if occasion shall arise.

Resolved, that the Chairman of this Meeting do cause Notice to be given by Advertisement in the Worcester Newspapers, and the Birmingham Herald, of the Alteration as to the time and place of holding of the Evesham Corn Market.

And that the Committee, at their discretion, do cause these Resolutions to be printed and distributed for the general Information of the Frequenters of the said Market.

And, lastly, it has been Resolved, that a Meeting of the Subscribers to the Market shall be convened by the said Committee, to be holden on the Evesham New Market-day in January, 1853, and in every subsequent year, for the auditing and passing their Accounts; when, after paying and providing for all liabilities relating to the said Market, the balance then in hand (if any) shall be invested strictly for the purpose of further Market Accommodation. The next Corn Market Committee to be elected on that day.

B. WORKMAN,

CHAIRMAN.

Mr. WORKMAN having retired from the Chair, it was moved by JAMES ASHWIN, Esq. and seconded by Mr. BARNES, that the Thanks of the Meeting be given to the CHAIRMAN and Mr. T. N. FOSTER, for the great trouble they have taken in obtaining the use of the Town Hall, and preparing and submitting the above Resolutions.

R. BULT, (LATE MAY) BOOKSELLER, PRINTER AND STATIONER, EVESHAM.

Notice of corn market, 1851.

EVESHAM

SALE OF SUPERIOR

HAWTHORN & ASH QUICK,

Potatoes, Bacon, Pigs, Casks, &c.

To be Sold by Auction,

BY

H. W. SMITH

On Wednesday next, the 26th of February, 1851,

A LARGE QUANTITY OF VERY SUPERIOR

5-year & 3-year-old Hawthorn

QUICK,

Ash and Crab Quick, Plants, Sixty Pots of Potatoes, Bacon, Two Fat Pigs, Garden Tools, Seeds, and other Effects, by order of the Executors, and on the Premises of the late MR. EDWARD SPIERS, Brier Cottage, Evesham.

INVENTORY.

Lot		Lot		Lot	
1	Four hampers and bench	23	Eleven sacks	46	Home-cured flitch of bacon, at per lb.
2	Two three-tine forks and shovel	24	Capital iron-bound half hogshead cask	47	Fat pig
3	Three ditto and spade	25	Ditto	48	Ditto
4	Two axes, two paddles and hoe	26	Quarter barrel	49	About sixty pots of potatoes, at per pot
5	Sheafpike, hedge hook & quick paddle	27	Ditto	50	About two thousand flower pots
6	Coal riddle, basket and setting pin	28	Eighteen gallon cask		
7	Ditto ditto	29	Ditto		Quick &c., in Brier Close Ground.
8	Grindstone and wateringpan	30	Twelve gallon ditto		
9	Three sieves	31	Salting lead	51	About fifty thousand 3-yr.-old hawthorn quick
10	Harrow	32	Round two-eared	52	About ten thousand ash quick
11	Chaff box and two knives	33	Round tub	53	About ten thousand crab quick
12	Radish board and trestles	34	Ditto	54	Plack of late plants
13	About two thrave of straw	35	Ditto	55	Ditto early ditto
14	Twenty-eight round ladder	36	Capital mash tub	56	Ditto red ditto
15	Twenty-four ditto	37	Tunpail and bucket	57	Ditto of transplanted quick
16	Wheelbarrow	38	Two buckets		
17	Ditto	39	Wash tub and ladepan		HILL GROUND, Near New Road.
18	Ditto	40	Large iron pot		
19	Dog kennel	41	Pair of steelyards, (56 lbs.)	58	Large quantity of very superior 5-yr-old hawthorn quick, in 2 convenient lots, as staked out
20	Hay knife, 7 and 14 pounds weights	42	Ditto, (30lbs.)	59	Ditto of ditto, 3-year-old ditto
21	Iron pig trough	43	Lot of garden seeds in lots	60	Ditto ditto, 3-year-old quick, adjoining in four lots, as staked out
22	Ditto	44	Home-cured flitch of bacon, at per lb.		
		45	Ditto ditto ditto		

Sale to commence at o'clock in the Afternoon.

The Auctioneer solicits particular attention to the above being of first-rate quality, and Sold without reserve, and will be offered in convenient Lots for purchasers; sufficient time will be given for the removal.

J. PEARCE, PRINTER, AND BOOK BRIDGE STREET, EVESHAM,

Sale notice of 1851.

14

ABOVE: Port Street before construction of Burford Road, and BELOW: old houses in Waterside (replaced by what is now the Park View Hotel).

ABOVE: Workman Bridge at time of erection and prior to the building of Avon Bridge house, and CENTRE: George Hunt and family in gardens of Avon Bridge house c 1880. BELOW: Lower Bridge Street, c 1880.

ABOVE: Upper Bridge Street, c 1880; LEFT: shops under the Booth hall (Round house) c 1870, and RIGHT: Market Place, c 1880 before enlargement of Public hall and showing the Old Red Lion Inn.

17

ABOVE: Rear of Old Red Lion Inn and adjoining premises in Market Place c 1880, and BELOW: the Mills, Evesham's main industrial area in Victorian times.

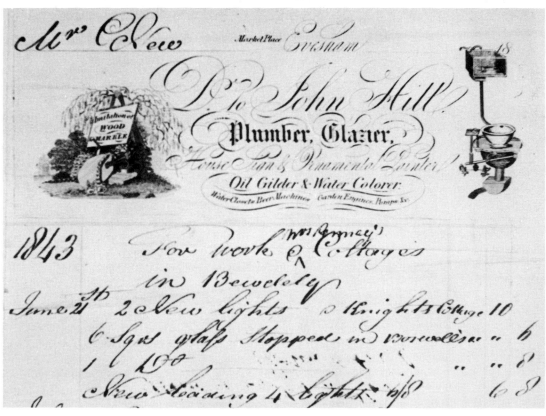

Tradesmen's bill heads of the 1840s.

*ABOVE: George May's old shop and printing works
in Market Place, c 1870 (now W.H.Smith Ltd.) and
BELOW: the Almonry, c 1895.*

ABOVE: Merstow Green from the Red Horse Inn
CENTRE: High Street before the private residences
were converted into shops. BELOW: The Cross Keys
in High Street before reconstruction.

*ABOVE: The High Street cobbles in the 1880s, and
BELOW: old Great Western railway station at
Evesham as originally constructed.*

LEFT: Herbert New: RIGHT: Prussia House on
Greenhill with Rev Bonaker in foreground;
BELOW: Former entrance drive to The Lodge on
Greenhill.

23

RIGHT: Some early Victorian traders' bills.
ABOVE LEFT: The Evesham Journal staff in 1888.
The founders of the paper, William and Henry Smith
are seated in the third and fourth seats in the second
row. BELOW: The town centre, c 1865. CENTRE
ABOVE: Harries & Co, (predecessors of Hamilton
& Bell Ltd - now Owen-Owen), and BELOW: Arthur
Marcus Hill Cheek.

*ABOVE: Bengeworth school girls' class 1896, and
BELOW: the Working Mens' Club leave Merstow
Green for an outing, c 1895.*

In the 1830s Evesham was a market town of about 4,000 souls and rapidly emerging from a static but prosperous period of its history, with important local industries in addition to its principal industry (which was market gardening). The town was beginning to benefit from the Evesham Town Improvement Act of 1824 under which common land, mostly in the Merstow Green area, could be sold to provide money to pave, cleanse, light, police and generally improve the appearance of this place and the lives of those living in it. Evesham then was an odd mixture of village and town, with its chapels and churches, its fine houses, orchards, farms, and market gardens, yet distinguished as the most commercially progressive town in the county outside Worcester, having its own Court of Quarter Sessions, Recorder, High Steward and Chamberlain and returning two members to Parliament. Birmingham and Manchester were unable to return even one member.

Many changes were to take place in the next decade. The Municipal Corporations Act of 1835 deprived the town of its Court of Quarter Sessions and overrode many of the provisions of the town's governing charter of incorporation, but for the first time gave the people the right to elect their own borough council and principal officers. The first election took place on 26 December 1835. Hitherto, admission to the council had been by invitation of the existing members, who filled vacancies as they arose, excluding nonconformists and people with radical views. The new Poor Law Act of 1834 made provision for the erection of a workhouse at Avonside and the appointment of a board of guardians. They would supervise the running of the institution, look after the needs of the poor and infirm, provide work for the able bodied, the apprenticeship of pauper boys to trade, and the preparation of girls for domestic service. The Marriage Act of the same year permitted nonconformists to celebrate their marriages in their own chapels, John Gibbs of Offenham lit the town with gas, and so by 1840 John Bentley was able to describe the town thus: 'The streets are kept clean and in good repair and are well lighted with gas and the shops are furnished with every necessity and luxury; so that Evesham is equal to most places in these constituents of comfort and civilisation; while its surpassing beauty and healthful atmosphere present strong attractions to visitants who will find excellent society here as the town and neighbourhood abound with respectable families whose mansions are seen in various directions enlivening and adorning the landscape.'

At this time many of the old half timbered and thatched dwellings in the main streets were being replaced with the brick mansions of the many merchants, bankers, professional men and well-to-do residents. Prince Henry's Grammar School, then on Merstow Green, was in a state of decline, largely because it did not teach what parents required their sons to learn, but John Deacle's charity school in Port Street was flourishing and turning out well educated boys for apprenticeship, many of whom later became leading members of the community. Their beautiful handwriting and figuring has never since been surpassed in Evesham schools in spite of (or because of) the so-called educational advances of modern times. Some provision was made for the education of those children who did not qualify for Prince Henry's or Deacle's, as Sunday schools and the National schools made progress.

June 1837 saw the death of King William IV, and the proclamation of the 18-year-old Victoria as Queen was made in the market place with the usual formalities; a Loyal address was sent from the borough. This was the start of the most peaceful, prosperous, and pro-

gressive period in British history. Her coronation in 1838 was an occasion for much public rejoicing in Evesham and, from a public subscription raised, the men of the town were regaled with a substantial dinner in the High Street, while later that day the wives and children were given tea and cakes. Similar festivities marked the wedding of the Queen in 1840 to Prince Albert of Saxe-Coburg-Gotha but on this occasion the food was eaten at home, the total supplied being 2,461 lb. of beef, the same number of threepenny loaves, and 592 buns for the children.

Almost every conceivable trade or craft was carried on in the town - not so much for consumption by the townsfolk as to meet the demands of those coming from far and wide to buy at the many fairs and markets for which Evesham was still famous. There were some quite substantial factories in the 1840s, and numerous mills and small workshops made parchment and nails, ground bones for fertilizers, and manufactured ropes and sacking. Gloving and stocking-knitting were the larger cottage industries. Riband weaving was introduced here in 1822 by John Clark of Coventry who erected a factory in Rynal Street, and silk throwing was introduced by Thomas Mann who built his factory in Littleworth Street. However, these trades were nearing their end as local industries by the middle of the century. Evesham had also lost its large shoe and woollen-cloth making industries, and with townspeople moving to growing industrial cities elsewhere, Evesham's industry was somewhat in decline. Hops were grown in Bengeworth and Hampton, and Samuel Amos carried on business as a hop merchant in Bridge Street. Mary Ansell, Sarah Lewis, Sarah Cull, and other ladies were busy making straw hats, and Charles Badger made hats in Bridge Street. His brother William made baskets there; Job Baylis, the then town crier, was a shoe maker; Evesham historian George May sold books, stationery, and patent medicines, and wrote, published, printed, and bound his history of Evesham in Bridge Street. William Spragg built boats at Bengeworth, Edward Goodall made parchment in Waterside and the needs of the people in the 1840s and 1850s were well supplied. The town was pretty well self-supporting, main imports being coal and the raw materials for keeping the manufactories going, most of this coming by river. It is remarkable that so many of our present day business names such as Burlingham, Goodall, Hodgetts, White, Wheatley, Huband and others were well known in the town in the 1840s, and some of them much before then. A directory of 1839 gives 19 butchers in Evesham, mostly in business in the Shambles, and one wonders if the old stories about most Evesham people being able to afford meat only once a week can be true. There were something like 50 public houses, but it must be remembered that many of the publicans and ale-house keepers carried on other businesses, and some only opened on market days and on the numerous fairs and public holidays. Other publicans worked on the land and left their wives or an employee to cope with the customers during the day time.

As the century progressed numerous parliamentary reforms, concerning, among other things, education, employment, and public health, had their effect. The penny post had arrived and various schemes for bringing the railways through Evesham were being discussed.

Before the railways eventually came in the 1850s the Greenhill area of Evesham was a quiet, almost rural part of the town with a few large mansions surrounded by ornamental gardens, orchards, and open fields. High Street finished at Almswood, which was for many years the home of first, Rev Timothy Davis and later Rev David Davis, both Unitarian ministers. Ascending Greenhill one would have seen on the east side Greenhill House, the residence of Herbert New, a local lawyer, author, poet, and Liberal, and the father

of Edmund Hort New, the well known artist who became famous for his book illustrations and drawings of the Oxford colleges. Further up and on the opposite side, was Prussia House (since demolished) which was the mansion of Rev W.B. Bonaker, the eccentric absentee vicar of Honeybourne, and arch-enemy of his neighbours the Rudges of Abbey Manor. The other large houses on Greenhill were the Croft and the large house which now houses Greenhill School (formerly, for many years, the grammar school), Eastfields House and, near the junction with Blayneys Lane, The Lodge, which had been the home of Robert Blayney the eminent lawyer and the town's Recorder. Opposite was Battlewell House (since demolished), and at the meeting of the roads on the borough boundary was the turnpike or toll house kept by Mr Masters.

Great and Little Hampton was in those days a separate parish and not part of the borough, and with a population in 1840 of under 300. Mrs Baselgett occupied Eastwick House, and John Lightbourn kept the Navigation Inn at Avonside and had a coal wharf opposite. He enjoyed a good trade from the commercial river traffic. The land was principally used for farming but later in the century, like most villages in the Vale of Evesham, it went over to market gardening and fruit growing. The Hampton farmers of this time were the Lunn, Preedy, Malin, Smith, Stanford, Staite, and Drinkwater families.

The great event of the century so far as the appearance of the town was concerned was the decision, after many meetings and lengthy negotiations, to erect a new bridge over the Avon in place of the oft rebuilt and repaired mediaeval bridge linking Bridge Street and Port Street, by then too narrow and dangerous due to increased volume of traffic. The work involved clearing away the numerous osier beds and obstructions mid-stream, the removal of the old and untidy wharves on the Hampton side of the old bridge, the straightening out and lining of the river banks, and the formation of the new pleasure gardens on the Bengeworth side. The bridge was completed in 1856 and the rest of the scheme by 1864, both the bridge and the gardens named after the untiring Henry Workman of Hampton, Mayor of Evesham and the man who got things done in those days. The Workman Gardens first came into use for the purpose of general public recreation and amusement in July 1864, when the Evesham flower show and regatta were held from there to celebrate the occasion. This was a great success and, to quote the *Evesham Journal* of that week, 'the feasibility of establishing an annual regatta at Evesham is henceforward removed from the region of doubt and the new bridge bore the heaviest human freight ever seen on it'. The old Bridge Inn, on the west side of what is now the Methodist church, was demolished at the same time. Apart from this the latter half of the century saw little enlargement or improvement of the town, which had for centuries consisted only of High Street, Vine Street, Merstow Green, Bridge Street, Port Street, Waterside, a few ancient side-streets leading off, and a scattering of outlying mansions and farmhouses.

In the 1880s the livestock markets had been cleared from the streets, leaving the widest High Street in the county, with its cobbled sidewalks and spacious pedestrian ways. The discontinuance of the street cattle markets caused the town council a perpetual problem - weeds came up so profusely between the cobbles. The fruit and vegetable markets stayed in High Street outside the Star hotel until the opening of covered markets. Mrs Henry Martin, writing in 1907, remembered well the old Evesham cattle markets: 'On these cobble-stones on fair-days was a motley crowd of men and beasts, for the market was held in the street. Here let my conservative mind own to an improvement! The smell on, say, the annual ram fair, which penetrated the drawing room and haunted our slumbers was - well, I need not dilate upon it! Some dear old ladies of my acquaintance on these

Mondays were so upset by the sight of the poor, harrassed, over-driven animals that they invariably "ordered their fly" early and spent the day out of sight and sound, at the then pretty rural village of Hampton.'

For news the town relied on market gossip, on *Berrow's Worcester Journal*, which had been circulating since 1690, and later on the *Evesham Journal* (1860) and the *Evesham Standard* (1888), these local papers becoming viable as the standard of literacy improved.

In October 1864 the Mayor, Thomas White, acting on the authority of the Privy Council, authorized the closing of all cattle, sheep, and pig markets as a precaution against the cattle plague which was ravaging the countryside. The following month saw the town's municipal elections, and feelings ran high, with a fair bit of intimidation from various quarters. There was much excitement, with cheering or booing, as the totals cast for the various candidates were announced from time to time during the day. A German band toured the town playing 'Hurray for the bonnets of blue', and the undecided prolonged their indecision whilst being plied with drink by supporters and agents. By mid-day the voting was brisk and the 'whites' were leading, but they were overtaken during the afternoon by the 'blues', who ultimately won with all three of their candidates. The figures were: G.Tredwell 264, F.C.Bicknell 257, M.Perry 240, T.New 227, E.Felton 213, and W.W.Brown 211. The Ballot Act of 1872 took away much of this excitement, as it provided, for the first time, for votes to be cast in secret, the returning officers announcing results from the town hall at the end of the day.

The new church of St Peter in Bengeworth was consecrated and opened on 7 September 1872 by the bishop of Worcester, and the church clock was subsequently presented by Mr Henry Burlingham, who lived opposite at Lansdowne.

Evesham was greatly honoured in 1875 when the 32nd annual meeting of the British Archaeological Association was held at the town hall. It lasted for five days, under the presidency of the Marquess of Hertford, with the Mayor of Evesham and His Royal Highness the duc d'Aumale as vice presidents. Special trains and carriages were arranged to take the 100 or so attending the meeting to the special places of interest in the Vale.

The cottage hospital in Briar Close was built in 1879 with funds publicly subscribed. The matron's report for 15 March 1880 reads: 'Admitted 1, discharged 0. Number in the house 3. Visitor of the week Mrs Hunt.'

The working men's club and institute on Merstow Green opened its doors in 1879 (Happy centenary!) and provided a good library, discussion groups, and leisure facilities. In the same year the master of the workhouse gave the following statistics to the Board of Guardians in one of his weekly reports: 'Men, able bodied 3, temporarily disabled 12, old and infirm 41. Women, able bodied 3, temporarily disabled 3, old and infirm 24. Children 22. Vagrants relieved during the week 23.'

A new turret with an illuminated clock with four dials was erected over the town hall in 1887 at a cost of £655, which was met by public subscription as a memorial of the Jubilee of Queen Victoria. This became known as 'Emma Morris', after the wife of Mayor Issac Morris. Rev George Head, sometime rector of Aston Somerville, presented a weather vane with wind indicator, barometer, and thermometer, which are still to be seen on the north wall of the town hall, and to mark the same occasion the Misses Burlingham presented a mural drinking fountain.

The coming of the railways in the 1850s and 1860s facilitated trade and travel and was of immense benefit to the town which, although it was already an important market-gardening town, was to become the centre of a much larger gardening community, as the

farms of the surrounding villages went over to gardening and fruit growing, with the ability to transport produce much greater distances quickly and in good condition. Although agriculture in England was generally in the doldrums in the second half of the century, the change-over from traditional farming to market gardening and fruit growing in the Vale ensured a high measure of prosperity for town and district.

By the third quarter of the 19th century the area of land under intensive horticulture was not much more than 1,250 acres, but by the end of the century it had risen to something over 10,000 acres, the pioneering James Myatt of Offenham leading the way with improved methods of cultivation on a field scale. To the families of Masters, Field, Cole, New, Grove, Andrews, and others, belong much of the credit for continuing and developing the enterprise.

There was considerable local competition in the growing of asparagus to perfection. In 1856 two growers, Joseph Grove and John Huxley, wagered two sovereigns on who could produce the heaviest hundred heads. The result was Grove 19½ lb. and Huxley 20½ lb. Evesham had the monopoly of early radish growing. Seed was usually sown in December or January and covered with straw in the early evening in frosty weather. Consignments from Evesham were dispatched by train late in the day to arrive in places like Manchester by 3 am the next day. It is recorded that in March 1880 one buyer alone dispatched 300 hampers of radishes by rail in one day.

1889 saw the fruit growers in a great deal of trouble with a particularly bad attack of caterpillars, which completely defoliated local orchards. As a result the Evesham Fruit Pests Committee was formed under the leadership of Joseph Masters. Many experts were brought in to advise, and active steps were taken to inform growers of the precautions necessary to prevent further catastrophes of this kind.

Disputes were frequent between growers and buyers in the latter half of the century as to what the local measure known as a 'pot' really was, since it varied from village to village, and in 1891 Harvey Hunt, who was the first to organize fruit and vegetable auctions in Evesham, brought out a standard which became universally accepted for the future, and a 'pot' would thereafter contain: apples 64 lb.; turnips 60 lb.; pears and plums 72 lb.; beans 40 lb.; cherries & currants 63 lb.; onions 64 lb.; parsley 20 lb.; potatoes 80 lb.; sprouts 40 lb.; gooseberries 63 lb.

Birds posed a major problem for the growers, and children were employed as bird minders in the 1880s at 3d. a day, with dinner and tea found for them on Sundays. The following bird minders' song, common to the Vale of Evesham, although remembered with various variations, was recorded by the late Mr F.W.Hallam:

> Ah! you nasty black-a-top,
> Get off my master's radish tops:
> He is coming with his long gun,
> You must fly and I must run.
> > Oh you hallo!
> > Eh you hallo!
> > Eh you hallo!
> Hallo, Hallo, Hallo, Ay.

Another old Evesham rhyme which might be worth remembering (if there are any elms left) was:

> When elm leaves are as large as a farden,
> Its time to plant kidney beans in the garden.

When elm leaves are as big as a shilling,
Plant kidney beans, if to plant 'em you're willing.
When elm leaves are as big as a penny
You must plant kidney beans if you're to have any.

The gardeners of Bewdley Street observed the annual custom of electing their own Mayor until well into the second half of the 19th century. This was preceded by drinks at the George and Dragon followed by the well established custom of placing the first choice for Mayor, usually drunk, on the back of a gardener's flat-bedded dray. He was then drawn up and down the street, with the object, if possible, of tipping him off into the ditch at the bottom of the street. If he was tipped he was not regarded as man enough, and the procedure was repeated with other candidates until one was found who satisfactorily qualified himself to hold the honourable position. The custom was eventually banned by the Watch Committee after a particularly notorious celebration.

Saint Thomas' day (21 December) was a special day for 19th century children of Evesham and continued to be observed well into the present century. Many older residents remember going round to the houses of the well-to-do to sing and dance for them and to receive gifts of fruit and cake, and sometimes money, with which to enjoy themselves better at the forthcoming Christmas. This was known as 'Thomasing'. The last known benefactor in Evesham was Mr Proctor Vernon Wadley of Durcott House in Bengeworth - there was always a great scramble for the oranges and pennies which it was his custom to dispense from a bedroom window.

The coming of the motor car towards the end of the century was, as elsewhere, received with repugnance in Evesham on account of the noise and dust and possible danger to life and limb. The vehicles were always breaking down, and the late Raymond Webb, a local pioneer motorist, recorded taking three days to get to Tewkesbury and back! The first garages were at the Crown Hotel yard and in the yard of the Fleece Inn, the latter garage first named 'The motor car stables'. The subsequent erection of the sign 'Garage' resulted in not a few people pointing out that the owner, Valentine New, should have spelt it Carage with a C! Nevertheless this was still the age of the bicycle which, although expensive to buy, offered considerable freedom of movement and, unlike the horse cost nothing to keep beyond the cost of occasional punctures and repairs due to bad roads. While a horse could not reasonably be expected to do more than 20 to 30 miles in a day, local cycling enthusiasts often knocked up 60 to 100 miles in a day, and on shopping days Evesham was full of country folk who had come in by 'cycle.

Goods and passengers were also carried to and from Evesham by carriers operating from the surrounding villages, the principal stopping places in Evesham being outside the Rose & Crown, the King's Head, the Royal Oak, and the Red Lion. Evesham was growing in importance as a shopping centre, turning many of the private residences in the main streets into shops, the owners moving out to the villages or to the outskirts of the town.

Although the upper and professional classes in the early and middle Victorian period were able to enjoy a good social life, the majority of the people found their social activities centred either around the churches and chapels or the inns and taverns, with little communication between the two. Although attendance at public houses was much frowned upon by the non-conforming communities it must be recognized that the inns and taverns, with their sickness and benefit societies and club nights, played an important part in the life of the working classes.

The Quaker chapel in Cowl Street, built in 1676, was active throughout the period, the

Baptist chapel in Cowl Street (in course of demolition as these words are written) was erected in 1788, the Unitarians had been in Oat Street since 1737, the Wesleyan Methodists had their chapel, built in 1808, in Chapel Street, and a breakaway group who called themselves the Reformed Wesleyans erected a chapel in the market place (since absorbed into Coulter's Garage) in about 1865.

T.J.S. Baylis, who spent many years researching information on the licensed trade in Evesham, established that early in Victoria's reign (in 1841) Evesham had four inns and posting houses, 28 public houses and taverns, and ten retailers of beer, one for every 100 of the adult population. We must of course have in mind that these facilities were mainly for those attending markets and fairs.

The first public library in Evesham was erected in the market place in 1824 and as the working population became more literate it was greatly enlarged, and the premises, under the style of the Literary, Scientific, and Mechanics' Institute, provided facilities for evening classes, adult education, lectures, and concerts. Numerous new societies came into being to provide leisure facilities, including the Dramatic Society in 1882, the Ladies' Choral Society in 1888, and the Operatic Society in 1902.

Discipline in the schools was good and punishments usually well deserved. Mr Gibbs of Bengeworth recalled that a stroke of the cane was known as 'custard', and he well remembered slow learners being made to stand in a corner wearing a paper cap bearing the word 'dunce'. It was also common for children to be made to stand in a corner on one leg and to be made to suffer other forms of indignity thought up by the teachers, which appear to have achieved the desired results. Mrs Eva Beck, in her book *Shut up the Puppets*, reported severe punishments at the grammar school when the then head, Dr Wilding, who had an uncontrollable temper, administered severe thrashings, and that on one occasion he met his match when he went too far with one boy, whose father, an auctioneer by profession, turned up at the school with a heavy knobbed walking stick and pursued the head with it, getting in numerous blows.

Although it must be accepted that the happy days of Victoria's reign stick in the memories of our most senior citizens more vividly than the unhappy ones, those who have recorded their way of life in Evesham seemed content with it, in the realisation that although there was a good deal of poverty in Victorian times the many charitable organizations functioning in the town, and the poor law system then in force, coped with the situation pretty well. On the whole they were perhaps better off than many in other parts of the country, and had beautiful surroundings in which to live. They have happy memories of their childhood days, of church and chapel and all the social life that went with it, of boating and fishing, skating on the frozen river, playing tip-cat, jack-in-the-rag-bag, hop-scotch, hoops, marbles, tops, and other street games. They remember the numerous concerts, musical evenings, penny readings, the annual regatta, the mop fair and travelling theatrical companies, German bands, dancing bears, picnics on Clarks Hill, the old cinemas, the 'Handcuffed King' and 'Professor Powsey' who dived off the Workman Bridge, flower shows, fetes in the Workman Gardens and at Abbey Manor, and much more besides. Certainly there was plenty going on in the town for all ages and one would need to read the *Evesham Journal* from number 1 onwards to get the full picture. There is no doubt that the people of Evesham during the reign of Victoria enjoyed a good standard of living and owed much to its enlightened town council, its squire, and its shrewd men of business.

MARTYR OF ALLAHABAD

The hearts of evesham people were stirred in 1857 when news came through that Arthur Marcus Hill Cheek, second son of Oswald Cheek, Evesham's then town clerk, had died from wounds sustained in the dreaded Indian mutiny. This young man of Evesham, who had been a pupil at Oxford House school in High Street, though barely 17 years of age, was an ensign in the Bengal native infantry, which until that time had been considered one of the most loyal. The regiment mutinied and massacred most of its officers, murdered the officers' wives and children, and occupied the fortress of Allahabad. Nine of Marcus's fellow ensigns were murdered outright, but Marcus managed to escape temporarily with severe head wounds. He crawled away and sought refuge, but was captured by a zemindar, a native landowner, who imprisoned him with others who had been found. Marcus was threatened with death unless he renounced his Christian faith and became a Mohammedan. While in the hands of the enemy Marcus saw a native Christian catechist being tormented and terrified into a recantation. This poor man had taken almost as much punishment as the human body could endure, and was weakened when Marcus cried out 'O my friend! Come what may, do not deny the Lord Jesus Christ'. Shortly afterwards the besieged garrison of Allahabad was relieved. Marcus was found and brought back to the fort, but he died the same evening and was buried in its covered way. The story of his heroic resistance to brutal ill-treatment and starvation at the hands of the enemy was told by fellow prisoners who survived, and a full account appeared in *The Englishman* of Calcutta on 24 June 1857, and in many newspapers in this country. His God-father, Lord Marcus Cecil Hill, Member of Parliament for Evesham in Queen Victoria's first Parliament, and later Comptroller of the Queen's household, wrote, in his letter of condolence: 'What a melancholy gratification it is to know that he was so much appreciated'.

COMMONS OF EVESHAM

1826 - 1830	Sir Charles Cockerell and Edward Protheroe
1830 - 1831	Sir Charles Cockerell and Lord Archibald Kennedy
1831 - 1835	Sir Charles Cockerell and Thomas Hudson
1835 - 1837	Sir Charles Cockerell and Peter Borthwick
1837 Feb	George Rushout Bowles (later known as Hon George Rushout)
1847 - 1841	Hon George Rushout and Lord Marcus Cecil Hill
1841 - 1847	Lord Marcus Cecil Hill and Peter Borthwick
1847 - 1855	Lord Marcus Cecil Hill and Sir H. P. Willoughby
1855 - 1865	Sir H.P. Willoughby and Edward Holland
1865 - 1867	Edward Holland and Lt Col James Bourne
1867 - 1880	James Bourne (Borough deprived of one member)
1880 - 1885	F.D. Dixon-Hartland (Evesham constituency merged 1885)
1885 - 1892	Sir Richard Temple
1892 - 1894	Sir E. A. H. Lechmere, Bt.
1895 - 1910	Colonel C. W. Long
1910 - 1935	Bolton M. Eyres-Monsell (later Viscount Monsell of Evesham)

Trade card and Worcestershire Agricultural
Society award of Joseph Gilbert, 1873.

ABOVE: Culls' Bakery - Upper Port Street, 1880
and BELOW: Workman Gardens, c 1890.

ABOVE: Lower Port Street, 1890, and
BELOW: Fleece Inn and cottages, Lower Bridge
Street, c 1890.

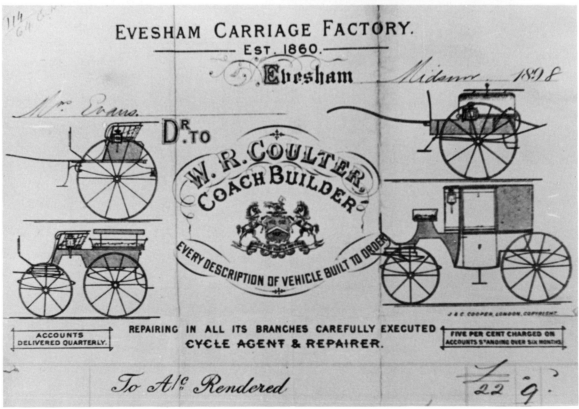

LEFT: Bridge Street, Messrs Badger's shop sign;
RIGHT: completed vehicles outside W.R. Coulter's
carriage works in the Market Place, and BELOW:
W.R. Coulter's bill-head, 1890.

ABOVE: Evesham Journal offices and J.C. Timms'
Hairdressing shop in Market Place. BELOW:
Isaac Morris's bill head, 1890.

[handwritten note at top:] William Russel has authority to go out ... of the 2 preachers during the quarter ... to go ... Rev Hyde to keep house June 14 ... Gibbs to Broadway on 21st June

George Cartwright *[signature]*

THE
WESLEYAN METHODIST
PLAN
OF
DIVINE SERVICES
IN THE
EVESHAM CIRCUIT.

From May 3rd to July 26th, 1896.

CIRCUIT STEWARDS.

MR. J. FOSTER, Evesham.
MR. F. ECCLES, Wyre.

FOREIGN MISSIONS

TREASURER: MR. J. FOSTER, Evesham.

SECRETARIES: { REV. BERTRAM COOPER, Campden.
{ MR. CAUDLE, Evesham.

CIRCUIT CHAPEL SECRETARY: MR. W. A. FISHER, Evesham

EDUCATION SECRETARY: REV. B. COOPER.

LOCAL PREACHERS' TRAVELLING FUND.
TREASURER: MR. A. T. HYDE, Evesham.

EVESHAM:
KNAPTON & MAYER, PRINTERS, BRIDGE STREET.

PRICE 2d.

PREACHERS' NAMES AN[D]

GEORGE CARTWRIGHT, Evesham
BERTRAM COOPER, Campden

G. Carter, Willersey

R. Gray, Bidford
G. Gibbs, Evesham
W. Pitts, Honeybourne
F. Eccles, Wyre
Jno. Fisher, Arrow
J. Hartwell, Willersey
J. Hobbs, Wyre
W. James, Bidford
F. Crossley, Admington
T. Neal, Quinton
J. Valender, Dunnington
J. Walton, Evesham
J. Halford, Willersey
C. Harris, Bidford
J. Alcock, Ilmington
A. Harris, Welford
A. T. Hyde, Evesham
H. Mayer, Evesham
J. Allard, Pebworth
J. Webb, Willersey
E. Harker, Hampton
W. Ingles, Willersey
T. Jackson, Pebworth
G. Haines, Evesham
A. Walton, Campden
Q. Read, Hampton
P. Squires, Pershore
T. Bryant, Aston Somerville

On Trial.

F. W. Pearson, Bruton.

J. I[...]

Sup[...]

D. [...]
D. A[...]

Fr[...]

A. V[...]
T. V[...]
J. L[...]
G. S[...]
J. N[...]
Jos.[...]
T. F[...]
R. E[...]
F. S[...]
D. H[...]
J. M[...]
A. V[...]
— C[...]
Jon.[...]
E. P[...]
C. C[...]
Sup[...]
To be [...]

*LEFT: Wesleyan Methodist circuit preaching plan
for 1896; ABOVE: Frederick Cox's advertisement
of 1890, and BELOW: T.W. Green's advertisement
of the same year.*

41

*ABOVE & OPPOSITE: Some late 19th century
traders' bill-heads. BELOW: Workmen of Henry
Masters weighing up, c 1899.*

PARIS HOUSE,
43. HIGH STREET,

Evesham Xmas 1893

The Trustees of Beadles Charity

Dr to Arthur Wheatley,

Maker of the Patent Hide Prize Medal Waterproof Boots & WATERPROOF COMPOSITION.

TRADE MARK.
ALSO BOOT MAKER BY APPOINTMENT TO HIS ROYAL HIGHNESS THE DUKE OF ALBANY AND TO THE MOST NOBLE THE MARQUIS OF HERTFORD

A Large Stock of Ladies, Gentlemen's & Children's Boots & Shoes ALWAYS ON HAND.

AGENT FOR ALL KINDS OF SEWING MACHINES.   5 PER CENT INTEREST CHARGED ON OVERDUE A⁄cs

1893   £   s   d

Sep 29 | To 30 pair of Boots @ 8/6 } Handsewn — } 12 15 0

EVESHAM INSTITUTE.

PENNY READINGS,

On Thursday Evening, March 14, 1867.

PROGRAMME.

Overture . . . . *Pianoforte.*

DRAMATIC SELECTION   Henry v. Acts iv. & v.   *Shakespere.*

    Mr. Herbert New, assisted by Messrs. **F. W.** Astley, W. Ballinger, F. Ballinger, John Churchill, B. George, F. Hollinshead, James Meddings, John Murrell, E. Purslow, H. Ward, & James Whitwell.

MR H. SMITH . Song   "Never mind the rest"   *Fase.*

MR. H. NEW   Reading   "Hallowed Ground"   . *Campbell.*

    Pianoforte Selection.

MR. H. NEW . Reading . "Tom the Chimney Sweep" *Kingsley.*

    "GOD SAVE THE QUEEN"

Reading to Commence at Eight.

LEFT: Penny readings programme 1867. RIGHT: Rev David Davis by E.H.New, 1897, and BELOW: Diamond Jubilee medal 1897.

44

PROGRAMME.

AT 8 o'clock on FRIDAY, DECEMBER 29th, and 2-30 o'clock on SATURDAY, DECEMBER 30th, will be acted the famous Comedy in 3 Acts, by the late T. W. ROBERTSON, entitled

"CASTE."

CHARACTERS—

Hon. George D'Alroy	Mr. OLIVER H. NEW
Captain Hawtree	Mr. E. D. LOWE
Eccles	Mr. HARRY J. SMITH
Sam Gerridge	Mr. H. HARTLEY SMITH
Dixon	Mr. DONALD WARNER
Marquise de St. Maur	Miss PIPER
Esther Eccles	Mrs. OLIVER H. NEW
Polly Eccles	Miss A. GILL SMITH

Act I.—The Little House in Stangate.—COURTSHIP.
(A lapse of eight months.)

Act II.—The Lodgings in Mayfair.—MATRIMONY.
(A lapse of twelve months.)

Act III.—The Little House in Stangate.—WIDOWHOOD.

There will be Intervals of Twelve minutes between the Acts.

Dramatic Society personnel 1899.

45

ABOVE LEFT: Advertisements from regatta programme 1898. ABOVE RIGHT: Cricket on Merstow Green by E.H.New, c 1890; BELOW RIGHT: bankers'cheques of the 19th century (Andrew Watton collection), and BELOW: cottages on east side of High Street, since demolished.

NOTICE.

We, whose Names are hereunto Subscribed, having formed an

ASSOCIATION, CALLED THE EVESHAM

ANGLER'S SOCIETY

FOR THE PROTECTION OF THE FISH IN

THE RIVER AVON.

And being either the Owners or Tenants of the several Fisheries herein after mentioned, or having otherwise obtained full Power and Authority from the several Persons who have any claim or right thereto: **DO HEREBY GIVE NOTICE** of our intention henceforth to prevent the Netting and Poaching which have been carried on illegally to a great extent for some time in the said Fisheries: therefore all Persons are cautioned not to use any kind or description of Nets, Engines, Wheels, Putcheons, Traps, Trimmers or Night Lines, for the catching or taking of Fish or Eels in the River Avon, from Harvington Weir to Chadbury Mill, as relates to the whole of the said River, or in the Waters called the Faulk Mill Brook, Hampton Brooks, and the Back Brook which latter adjoins Glover's Island.

Every Person Trespassing, after this Public Notice, will be Prosecuted according to Law.

And whoever will give information to MR. EADES, the Solicitor to the Society, or to MR. BARNES, the Treasurer, of any Person or Persons Trespassing with Nets, Engines, Wheels, Putcheons, Traps, Trimmers or Night Lines, so that he or they may be convicted thereof, shall on such conviction, receive from the Society

TEN SHILLINGS REWARD.

But we give this further Notice, that our principal object is to secure Sport for Anglers, therefore all Persons will have free access to the River, (except on Sundays,) for the purpose of Fishing with the Rod and Line, the consent of the occupier of the Land adjoining the said River or Brooks being first obtained. And as the Association is for the benefit of the Public generally, they expect the assistance of the Public in securing sport to the fair Angler in one of the best breeding Rivers in the Kingdom.

EDWARD JOHN RUDGE, — President.
ROBERT BLAYNEY, — Vice President.

John Ashmore	John Proctor Dunn	Thomas Furley Smith
Richard Ashwin	George Eades	John Allen Stokes
William Barnes	John Marshall	Thomas White
Charles Best	Oswald New	Benjamin Workman
Proctor Clark	John Pitts	Henry Workman

Rules and Regulations of the Evesham Angler's Society.

1. That the subscription of each Member be not less than Ten Shillings and Sixpence a year, the subscription to commence on the first day of June in each year; and that every new Member be elected either at a general Meeting, or by the Committee of Management.

2. That no person shall be allowed to use any kind of Net, Night Line, or Trimmer: but the Members of the Association will have the liberty of putting down Putcheons or Traps for the purpose of taking Eels.

3. That no Trolling or Fishing of any kind be allowed between the 20th of February and the 20th of May.

4. That every Member shall have the liberty of Fishing with two Rods and Lines, and not more at the same time.

5. That all persons living within the Borough of Evesham, the Parishes of Norton and Lenchwick, Offenham, the Hamlet of Aldington, and Parish of Great and Little Hampton, shall be allowed to Angle provided they conform to the Rules of the Association, otherways they will be prosecuted as Trespassers.

6. That any person visiting Evesham, or either of the Parishes before mentioned, for the purpose of Angling, may obtain a Card of leave from the Treasurer.

7. That any Member wilfully transgressing either of the above Rules, shall be liable to expulsion from the Society.

8. That a Committee of seven Members of the Asso-

ciation be chosen to manage the affairs of the Society, three to be a Quorum.

9. That a Meeting of the Members generally, shall be held on the first Monday in June, and the first Monday in December in each year, for the purpose of auditing the accounts of their Treasurer, and for the business connected with the Association.

10. That MR. BARNES be appointed to catch, or cause to be caught, live Baits for the Members of the Association, between Evesham Mill or Weirs, and the Bridge. And he is hereby empowered to authorise any person to seize all Nets, Engines, Wheels, Putcheons, Traps, Trunks, Hard Wheels, Trimmers, or Night Lines, that may be used, set, or laid down in the aforesaid Fisheries.

Pearce, Printer, Evesham.

Notice of formation of Anglers' society

BOROUGH OF EVESHAM.

CATTLE PLAGUE.

BY AUTHORITY of ORDERS of the LORDS of HER MAJESTY'S MOST HONOURABLE PRIVY COUNCIL, bearing date respectively the 24th day of MARCH, and the 26th day of MAY, 1866, made in pursuance of several Acts of Parliament, therein mentioned, and referred to; the Committee to which the Local Authority, under the said Order, has delegated all the powers thereby conferred upon such Local Authority, BY THIS NOTICE, declare as follows:—

"That with a view to prevent the spreading of the disorder, generally designated as "The Cattle Plague," **it is expedient,** until further Notice, **to prevent the removal** of any Bull, Bullock, Cow, Ox, Heifer, or Calf, to any Market or Fair within the said Borough, and also to prevent the removal of any such animal, *for any purpose whatever*, within the jurisdiction aforesaid, without the Licence of one of the persons hereafter named.

"That no Animal shall be brought into the said Borough from any other place whatever, without the Licence authorised by the said Orders in Council."

The following persons are hereby appointed and authorised to grant the Licences aforesaid, and all such other Licences as are necessary under the said Order of the Lords of the Privy Council, namely:— ANTHONY MARTIN, Esq., Mayor; Mr. Alderman BURLINGHAM, Mr. Alderman WHITE, and Mr. Councillor ALLARD.

Any person in anywise offending in the premises will for every such offence forfeit any sum not exceeding **TWENTY POUNDS,** which the Justices before whom he or she shall be convicted of such offence, may think fit to impose; or other the penalties specified in the said Order of the Lords of the Privy Council.

Provided always that any animal free from the said disorder may pass through the jurisdiction aforesaid, while in course of removal from one part of the county of Worcester to any other part thereof, by virtue of a Licence granted by some Justice of the Peace for the said County, in pursuance of the Orders in force in such County.

Made this 23rd day of June, 1866.

OSWD. CHEEK,
Town Clerk, and Clerk to the said Local Authority and Committee.

W. & H. SMITH, Machine Printers, Evesham.

BOROUGH OF EVESHAM.
CORPORATION SWIMMING BATH.

HOURS FOR BATHING.

FOR FEMALES:

Daily (except Sundays and Wednesdays) - 6 a.m. to 12.30 p.m.

Wednesdays, 6 a.m. to 12.30 p.m. & 2 p.m. to 4 p.m.

Sundays · · No Bathing.

FOR MALES:

Daily (except Sundays and Wednesdays) - 2 p.m. to 9 p.m.

Wednesdays · · 4 p.m. to 9 p.m.

Sundays · · 6 a.m. to 9 a.m.

The Baths will be Closed during all other hours of the day.

CHARGES.

For every Person admitted to the Bath (whether Bathing or not), except on Saturdays · · · · · · · · **2d.**

On Saturdays admission to Bathers (except to Dressing Boxes, which will be charged 2d. each) · · · · · · **FREE.**

For a Single Season Ticket (not transferable) · · **FIVE SHILLINGS.**

For a Family Season Ticket (not transferable), to admit Parents and Children of a Family only · · · **TEN SHILLINGS.**

ADMISSION TICKETS, and on Saturdays DRESSING BOX TICKETS, must be obtained on entering the Bath of the Attendant, from whom Season Tickets can also be purchased. All Tickets must be produced, on demand, to the Attendant. Season Tickets are available until the end of the Bathing Season for which they are issued, terminating at a date to be fixed by the Town Council.

Drawers or suitable dress to be worn by Males, and the usual dress by Females, while Bathing.

The Attendant shall see that order and decency are observed in the Bath, and that there is no overcrowding. Any Person misconducting himself (or herself), will be excluded.

BY ORDER,

THOS. COX, Town Clerk.

Evesham, June 1st, 1899.

W. & H. SMITH, Limited, "Journal" Printing Works, Evesham.

Corporation baths notice of 1899.

UP.	WEEK DAYS.								SUNDAYS	
	1&2	1,2,3	Par.	1&2	1,2,3	1&2	1&2	1&2	1&2	Par. 1,2,3
Wolverhampton	...	...	7 40	..	..	1210	1 25	4 30	7 5	7 50 3 50
Dudley	...	...	8 5	..	..	12 5	1 48	4 45	7 25	8 15 4 15
Birmingham, Snw-hill.	..	..	7 25	..	..	1155	..	4 0	7 5	.. 3 30
Dudley.............	...	...	8 15	..	..	1235	1 50	4 35	7 30	8 25 4 20
Stourbridge..........	6 20	..	8 43	..	..	1 0	2 11	5 8	7 52	8 49 4 40
Hagley	..	..	8 51	..	..	1 7	2 18	5 16	7 58	8 56 4 47
Churchill...........	..	..	8 56	..	..	F	..	5 24	...	9 34 55
Kidderminster	6 34	..	9 5	..	..	1 19	2 30	5 31	8 9	9 12 5 5
Hartlebury	..	..	9 18	..	..	1 32	2 41	5 43	8 19	9 28 5 15
Droitwich	6 53	..	9 32	..	..	1 44	2 53	5 57	8 31	9 42 5 30
Fearnal Heath	..	..	9 40	..	..	1 51	..	..	..	9 50 5 40
Worcester........arr.	7 5	..	9 50	..	..	2 0	3 5	6 10	8 45	10 0 5 50
Hereford	..	..	8 20	..	9 40	1235	..	4 40	..	... ..
Malvern	..	..	9 23	..	1040	1 32	..	5 38	..	9 15 5 30
Worcester....M..dep.	7 10	..	10 0	..	..	2 15	..	6E25	9 25	1010 6 0
Pershore	7 23	..	1015	..	..	2 32	..	6 42	9 42	1030 6 15
Fladbury............	..	..	1023	..	..	2 40	..	6 50	9 47	1037 6 22
Evesham	7 38	7E55	1033	1050	..	2 50	..	7 1	9 55	1045 6 30
Honeybourne	*	8 5	1043	11 3	..	3 0	..	7 14	..	1057 6 40
Honeybourne	..	8 10	..	11 5	...	5 0	..	7 17	∴	.. ...
Long Marston......	..	8 16	..	1112	...	5 6	..	7 24	..	.. ..
Milcote	..	8 22	..	11..		5 13	..	7 31	..	.. ..
Stratford-npon-Avon	..	8 37	..			5 23	..	7 41	..	1020 6 5
Warwic..	..	9 5..				9..				11 9 6 46
										5 6 53

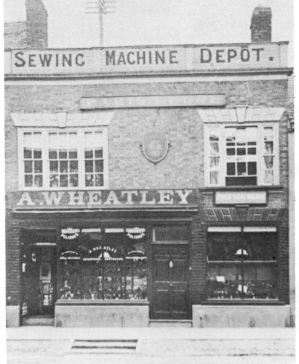

ABOVE: Extract from Evesham Journal Railway timetables for 1867. BELOW LEFT: A. Wheatley's shop on west side of High Street, demolished 1903, (now Linbar) and RIGHT: butter wrapping paper of S.W. Smedley. Mr Smedley's business grew to become one of the nation's largest fruit and vegetable canning businesses.

Hampton Street scene, c 1890.

High Street looking south, c 1880.

Vegetable market in High Street, c 1885.

THE FRENCH CONNECTION

Henri-Eugene-Philippe-Louis d'Orleans, duc d'Aumale, who was the fourth son of Louis-Philippe, the last King of France, came to live at Wood Norton Hall in 1857, and members of the royal house of Bourbon-Orleans occupied the property and other large houses in the area, including Craycombe House, until 1912, when the estate of some 4,000 acres was sold by his nephew, and successor as head of the royal house, Louis-Philippe-Robert, duc d'Orleans. During this period of occupation the family were visited by many of the royal families of Europe to whom they were related, and by members of our own royal family.

Of the more important of the 1860s visitors was Edward Prince of Wales, who came in 1867 for a few days' hunting with the duc d'Aumale, who at that time was president of the Worcestershire Hunt and had often entertained the prince in earlier days at Chantilly. The prince was accorded a right royal welcome by the people of Evesham, who turned out in great strength to be present at Evesham station to witness the arrival and departure of the prince and his party. An official reception committee was formed, and a guard of honour presented by the Evesham Rifle Corps under Captain Bullock. On arrival the prince was introduced to the Mayor, Mr W.T. Allard, and other local dignitaries, and was presented with a loyal address prepared on behalf of the people of Evesham, which cited the fact that the town's charter of incorporation had been granted at the request of a former Prince of Wales, Prince Henry, son of James I. The band played 'God bless the Prince of Wales,' and the royal party left for Wood Norton with the duc d'Aumale in his open landau drawn by four horses. During the prince's visit he was seen on many occasions and it is said that while hunting with the Worcestershire hounds on Bredon Hill he was thrown from his horse when endeavouring to jump a wall.

The visit in 1904 of King Carlos of Portugal and Queen Marie-Amelie, who was a sister of the duc d'Orleans, was an event which stirred up considerable interest in the town. He had come to Wood Norton for a few days' shooting, a pastime which he and the duc greatly enjoyed. The registers of births for that year show several Evesham boys christened Carlos.

November 1907 saw the wedding at Wood Norton of Princess Louise d'Orleans, a sister of the duc d'Orleans, to Prince Charles de Bourbon. This was attended by kings and queens, princes and dukes of Spain, Portugal, Russia, France, Belgium and Bavaria, and representatives of many other European countries, with all their attendants, bodyguards, servants, and a contingent from the bridegroom's regiment, the Pavian Hussars, he being a general in the Spanish army. As King Edward VII, who was known to be partial to the French, was unable to attend due to his engagement in the entertainment of Kaiser William of Germany and others at Windsor, he was represented by Princess Beatrice of Battenburg, whose daughter, also present, was Victoria Eugenie, the Queen of Spain who, with her husband King Alfonso XIII, had narrowly escaped assassination on their own wedding day the previous year.

The religious ceremony at Wood Norton was preceded early the same morning by a civil ceremony at the old iron Catholic church, which stood near the site of the present Catholic church. This iron building had previously been in Magpie Lane (Avon Street) and, after the building of the new Catholic church, was moved to Pershore, where it still stands in a builder's yard.

The presence of the French royal family in the district proved of great benefit to the people of Evesham.

Bridge Street during Royal wedding celebrations
1907.

53

ABOVE LEFT: The bride, Princess Louise d'Orleans and RIGHT: The bridegroom, Prince Charles de Bourbon-Siciles. CENTRE: The King and Queen of Portugal; BELOW (left and right): the Duc and Duchesse d'Orleans and CENTRE: Her Majesty the Queen of Portugal and HRH Princess Louise of France visiting Evesham Hospital, 30 November 1907.

54

EVESHAM 1900

What was the Evesham of our parents and grandparents like? Was it much different to the Evesham we know today? The answer seems to be that changes have been little, so far as the appearance of the town is concerned, compared with many towns, and some say 'hurray for that'! Let us take an imaginary stroll through the town at the turn of the century starting at Bengeworth Elm. The old elm tree standing at the point where the road forks left for Offenham gave its name to Elm Road and for many years the general area around Prospect House, the fine Georgian residence at our starting point, built by George Day, an Evesham lawyer and banker in the 18th century. Muzio Clementi, the famous Italian-born pianist, composer, and pianoforte manufacturer, died at Elm Lodge on 10 March 1832. His Will of 2 January 1832 describes him as 'late of Lincroft House near Lichfield in the County of Stafford but now of Evesham in the County of Worcester'. He is believed to have been in Evesham for only a few months.

Passing down Elm Road one would see Ivy House on the right, which was at one time an inn, and George Hunt's brickyard on the left, in the three-cornered field with the brickyard cottages at the junction with Badsey Lane, known as Bishops Corner. At the bottom of Elm Road was the site of the old toll house, the new church of St Peter, and the drinking fountain and horse trough provided by Henry Burlingham in 1884 to mark the occasion of the opening of the town's water works. Entering Port Street, Lansdowne (now council offices) was then the residence of the Misses Burlingham, and on the right of Elm Road and Port Street a vast area of land was in course of development, comprising Kings Road, Northwick Road, etc., - to be known to local residents as New Bengeworth - and all built on what was formerly Lord Northwick's estate in Evesham. A little further down was Church Street, much as it is today. The old National schools there were still in use for a variety of purposes and remained of great benefit to the parish until the Church House was built in Broadway Road in 1922/23. The site of the old parish church had a much higher wall around it than it has today and many more gravestones. Next was The Orchards, which became the home of the Masters family for many years. The Owletts, and then Durcott House, home of Proctor Vernon Wadley, the well known historian, who lived there from 1879 until his death in 1913. His obituary described him as an antiquarian with no equal in the County of Worcester. T.W.Beach & Sons, who had previously carried on their business at Toddington and elsewhere, erected their then up-to-date factory and offices in Church Street in 1906, and the business has ever since provided much employment and benefit. Church Street led on to Owletts End and to Coopers Lane, which was virtually as it is today, the principal residence being the Mansion House (now the Evesham Hotel) on the site of the mediaeval mansion of the Watson family. The property with 100 acres of land was sold to Thomas Watson in 1537 on the dissolution of Evesham Abbey. The house was subsequently enlarged and rebuilt by the famous Dr Thomas Beale Cooper.

A walk up various passage ways leading off Port Street would reveal Ralph Stanton's bakery, the Vine Brewery of Tommy Glasbrook, which still stands, Thomas Clements's rope and twine factory with its long rope walk, Frederick Wheeler the bill poster and town crier, and many others. Many of the old public houses of Port Street had disappeared by this time but we still had the Talbot kept by Mrs Pitman, the Swan by Frank Holder, the Bear by William Bailey, the Old Angel by Walter Candy, the New Angel by Sarah Ellis, and the Woolpack by Charlie Evans. Many of these publicans were still brewing their own beer and cider.

Among the old family businesses then carried on in Port Street were Fowlers the furnishers, who later went to High Street, Webbs the butchers and Wheatleys the furnishers (who are both still in business), Fosters the grocers, Pumphreys the chemists, and many others long since gone. Deacle's school was nearing the end of its days and was later to become a picture house, a club, and the labour exchange. A walk round the backs of the Port Street premises today will give a good indication of the amount of small businesses carried on, many of the old buildings, barns, and workshops still remaining. In The Leys and Castle Street area were Tipper's parchment works, behind the present Regal Cinema Gilbert's agricultural machinery works, the Salvation Army barracks, gardeners' cottages and sheds, Spragg's boat yard, with the adjoining public slipway where the gardeners washed their carts and in dry seasons collected water for the land. At the bottom of Port Street on the right was Bridge House, the residence of Dr Harry, later Miss Greenwood's Hotel Bonaire, later still the tax office and now Burlingham's showrooms and offices.

In Waterside were a few residential properties and the Northwick Arms, many of the old businesses and coal wharves having disappeared following the discontinuance of commercial traffic on the river and the formation of the Workman Gardens. Burlingham's yard, as always, was a hive of activity, and almost everything in the way of agricultural machinery, ironmongery, coal and tools could be obtained there.

Passing over the bridge we would come to Avon Bridge House on the left, erected in the early 1860s by George Hunt on the site of older property and of a timber yard, which he had purchased from the Evesham bridge trustees after the erection of the bridge. Next was the Golden Fleece Inn with adjoining cottages and a large yard behind, where George Brearley set up his first mineral water factory in 1885, and where Sinclair's theatre once operated. Opposite was Tom Evans' grocery shop and the site of an old coal wharf known as Avon Bank, which was soon to become the site of the new Methodist church opened in 1907. Mill Street led to what had been the centre of Evesham's larger manufacturing industries. In this part of the town were the sites of the former shoe making, milling, and leather industries. Although flour milling continued into the present century, the main buildings eventually came into the occupation of the English Concentrated Produce Co Ltd., which was engaged in the manufacture of Evesham sauce and the preservation of fruit and vegetables, but this venture eventually failed and the whole of the mills, cottages, and premises were sold off by auction in 1925 to become the meat processing factory of Collins Brothers (now Robirch). The Mill Street tannery was still in operation in the early years of the century; cottages there occupied by members of the staff, and for some reason known as 'Rats' Castle', have since been demolished as they jutted out into the road and impeded traffic.

Shakespeare's Avon or, to use its proper name, the Warwickshire Avon, has played an important part in Evesham's history, life, commerce, and communications, and is the town's main attraction, with practically all amenity land and recreational areas along its banks. The coming of the railways, with the inevitable transfer of cargoes from the rivers and canals, saw a rapid decline in the commercial importance of the river. The upper navigation between Evesham and Stratford became vested in the Oxford, Worcester and Wolverhampton Railway, later the Great Western, who discontinued taking tolls and allowed the locks to fall into decay. This had had its effect on the lower navigation between Evesham and Tewkesbury, which saw a rapid decline in income as most traffic wished to go beyond Evesham, so by the turn of the century there was virtually no commercial traffic, but in its place had come pleasure boating.

Charles Byrd ran river trips from the west bank near the Fleece Inn and later from the Tower View Cafe on the east bank. Sidney Spragg's boatyards were at the bottom of the Leys and in the lower Abbey Park, and he was succeeded in business by Walter Collins. Frank Malins had the New Bridge boating business in Avonside, and Sam Groves developed the Avon Bridge boatyard and tea gardens and in later years took over the Tower View Cafe. His later vessels the Hurley and the Gaiety were popular, but many older people will remember well the Lillybird and Diamond Queen of Charles Byrd, and the smaller boats of the other proprietors. Only the Gaiety now survives as a pleasure craft, and this old boat has quite a history. It originally worked under steam on the Thames and was brought to Evesham in 1929 via Reading, the Kennett and Avon canal, and into the Severn and Avon via Gloucester and Tewkesbury. Fred Lewis and party, who brought the boat, had to negotiate 110 locks, most of which they had to operate themselves.

The main event on the river from 1897 and for over 50 years thereafter was the Whit Monday regatta of the Evesham Rowing Club which was popular with crews from all over the country and earned the title 'The Henley of the Midlands'.

Bridge Street today has no licensed house but in 1900 the Crown, which one hopes will soon re-open, the Duke of York, and the Old Volunteer opposite the Round House, were well frequented.

Harry J.Smith and William Smith and Geoffrey and Oliver New practised law in Bridge Street, with Allen and Horace Haynes practising medicine nearby, and opposite were Knapton & Mayer the printers and booksellers, Rightons the auctioneers, and the Capital & Counties Bank. Many of the old family businesses of 1900 were still going strong 40 or more years later and of these one can mention E.W.Izod's the bakers, Ward & Son the jewellers, West's the clothiers, Strawson's the drapers, and Millward's shoe shop. Thomas Badger's business as a hat maker, which had functioned in Bridge Street for almost a century, still displayed its metal top-hat sign, which caught the eye and later appeared over the shop of Harrell & McHugh. Badger got into a good deal of trouble on one occasion by printing the words 'the only legitimate hatter in Evesham' on his bill-heads!

The ancient Cowl Street was of some importance at this time with its Baptist chapel and Quaker meeting house, its adult school and coffee tavern, various small businesses, the Golden Hart Inn (now the Golden Heart), and some private houses. The half timbered building at the Four Corners, known now as Shakespeare's Rest, was in pretty bad shape, and we are fortunate that it has survived. Passing through the Four Corners we would have come to the old Methodist chapel and minister's residence in Chapel Street, and in Oat Street the Green Dragon, Ashley's coach-building works, the Unitarian chapel, and what was then the new police station and magistrates' court, now part of the Wallace House complex.

The market place was still busy. William Salmon kept the Red Lion Inn; W.R.Coulter's coach-building and cycle works prospered, keeping up with the times and going into the motor car business. The *Evesham Journal* had their business where W.H.Smith Ltd. now operate, and the Evesham Club occupied the upper rooms. Whitford's the tobacconists and others occupied the ground-floor shops in what was then called the Booth Hall, now known as the Round House. The Maiden's Head, leading into Vine Street, was then called the Plough, and this street, formerly the pig market, was little different from today, many of the old cobbles still to be seen peeping through the modern tarmac surface of the foot-paths. Vehicles could then go no further than the Vauxhall Inn and Merstow Green, as Abbey Road and the Abbey Bridge had not been constructed. Eades & Son had their law

offices in the eastern part of the Almonry, and various families occupied the remainder of the building. Merstow Green was then common land and mostly grassed over and surrounded by the homes of market gardeners. The old Grammar School premises were occupied as a drill hall and a working men's club. To the south of the green was the vicarage (recently demolished to make way for the new health centre), to the west the Green school, and to the north the Trumpet Inn (not the old one where Brooke's restaurant now is, nor the present one, but one which existed between the closing of the old one and the building of the present one).

Like Bridge Street, High Street housed many of the leading families of the town, and many old and modern businesses, some of which were to survive for another 40 years, including Liley's the corn merchants, Salisbury's restaurant, and Hamilton & Bell's, the law firm of Byrch Cox & Sons, Yates's seed shop, Alcock's music shop, Carrick's the tobacconists, and others. Drs Martin & Slater practised where the Clifton (formerly the Scala) cinema now stands, with Trinder's fancy repository and Espley's the builders nearby, the present 'bus station being where the fruit and vegetable markets were held. The finest building in High Street, known as Dresden House, was then a school for young ladies and had in its grounds an unusual summer house called The Temple, a detached column surmounted by a weather vane, and an enormous carved fireplace bearing the arms of the Borough of Evesham, which was taken out of the town hall in 1728 when the present council chamber was formed. The summer house contained some fine panelling of the Tudor period, believed to have come from the private apartments of the abbot of Evesham.

The tree-lined High Street was much admired by visitors and had surprisingly few public houses, but those that remained were large and popular, including Sladden & Collier's Star Vaults, the Rose & Crown run by William Partridge, the Cross Keys by James Wood, the King's Head by Eustace Meadows, and the Railway Hotel by John Smith. At the end of High Street were the newish cattle and vegetable markets, the railway stations, and the nearby sawmills, and on the east of lower Greenhill the new housing estate comprising Victoria Avenue, Cambria Road, Princess Road, and Windsor Road, and going up Greenhill we would see the present Greenhill school, which was then Prince Henry's Grammar School and which, whilst at this location, produced such fine scholars as E.A.B.Barnard, MA., FSA., FRHist.S., who, as Evesham's leading historian of his day, became an Honorary Freeman of the Borough, and Henry Fowler, who later became Sir Henry, the famous designer of the Royal Scot and many other locomotives. Greenhill became the residential area of the upper crust.

Great and Little Hampton had by this time seen a lot of new building, particularly in the Pershore Road, and its population had almost trebled since 1840. It had its own railway station, which became known as Bengeworth because there were so many other places in England called Hampton, and the stationmaster at the turn of the century was Martin Wilson. Its National schools were built in 1873 with accommodation for 190 children, with Miss Starck as mistress-in-charge in 1900. The Navigation Inn at Avonside had by this time changed its name to the Crown Inn and was kept for many years by Harry Leech. It has since reverted to its former name. Charles Burlingham lived at Eastwick House, Joseph Greenways Knapp was vicar, William Girvin master of the workhouse, and T.W.Butler, a veterinary surgeon, Lord of the Manor.

The principal Eversham landowners in 1900 were Edward Charles Rudge, who was Lord of the Manor of Evesham, Lady Northwick, Francis Darwin, the Trustees of Mrs Lord and Captain H.R.M.Porter of Birlingham.

THE CENTURY GIVES WAY

*ABOVE: Prospect House, Elm Road; BELOW:
New Bengeworth in course of development.*

INSET: Junction of Elm Road with Port Street.
ABOVE: St Peters, Bengeworth; BELOW: Charles
Webb the Port Street butcher with his family and
staff, c 1900.

*Three views of John Foster's shop in Port Street
showing expansion over the years.*

LEFT: Hampton House; RIGHT: Crown Inn,
Hampton; CENTRE: Bengeworth (Hampton) station,
(photo: F. Cox) and BELOW: Spraggs boatyard,
lower Abbey Park.

ABOVE: Tower View Cafe, Avonside; CENTRE:
Workman bridge from Spragg's Lower Leys boatyard;
BELOW: S.J.Grove's tea gardens.

*ABOVE: The Diamond Queen; CENTRE: E.C.P. Ltd
bill-head; BELOW: Caudle Brothers, outfitters of
Bridge Street.*

Gardeners taking produce to market.

LEFT: Upper Bridge Street; BELOW: Crown Hotel,
Bridge Street; RIGHT ABOVE: E.W. Izod's shop,
Bridge Street; CENTRE: Ward & Son, Bridge Street,
and BELOW: corner of Mill and Bridge Streets.

*ABOVE: F.H.Alcock's music shop, Bridge Street,
Left to Right: Alfred Spratley, Frank Finch, Frank
Hubert Alcock (premises now Cheltenham and Glou-
cester Building Society); and LEFT: Evesham Journal
buildings on corner of Bridge Street and Market Place.
RIGHT: Church-yard cottages looking towards Vine
Street.*

67

ABOVE: Tudor House facing church-yard (now Coulters' workshops); BELOW: Market Place after enlargement of Public Hall.

ABOVE: The Plough Inn, Vine Street, (now called The Maiden's Head) and BELOW: chips at Evesham 'mop' fair.

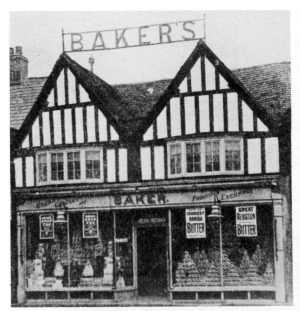

LEFT: Bakers' Stores, Vine Street (now Leamington Spa Building Society), RIGHT: Felton & Son, Vine Street (now The Falconry), and BELOW: funeral bier made at Coulters' Carriage Works in Market Place.

ABOVE: Vauxhall Inn, Vine Street; BELOW: the Trumpet Inn, Merstow Green (Herbert Pettit Landlord).

ABOVE LEFT: Hamilton & Bells, High Street and BELOW: The Great Western Station, 1905. CENTRE: J.G. Billings, High Street; ABOVE RIGHT: timber arriving at Evesham sawmills; CENTRE: many of the pictures in this book were from Fred Gegg's camera; BELOW: blossom time on Greenhill.

Products of Rowlands Brewery, Bewdley Street.

ABOVE LEFT: Ginger beer bottles made for J.F.Kingzett (from 1896-99); G.Brearley (From 1884); RIGHT: beer bottle used by J.T.Williams, Vine Street, (now King Charles Inn); BELOW: beer bottles made for: Rowlands, Bewdley Street; Sladden & Collier, Brick Kiln Street; W. Cooke, Bewdley Street & Bengeworth; Baylis & Son, Port Street.

Mineral water bottles made for: Thomas New, Bridge Street; George Brearley. Fleece Yard and The Leys; W. Lean, Port Street; G.Pumphrey, Port Street; T.E. Doeg, Bridge Street.

Some early Evesham holiday postcards.

WAR AND PEACE

The first four decades of the 20th century were to be the most eventful in our national history, with wars and rumours of wars, inventions for good or evil, social and other changes, and of course Evesham was affected by them all in greater or lesser degree.

The news of the death of Queen Victoria in 1901 came as a sad blow to the people in spite of her great age. A contemporary account reported groups of people standing in Evesham's streets discussing the event, the bell tolling in the bell tower, the shops closed and social activities at a standstill. The following day a muffled peal was rung, flags were lowered to half mast, and the duc d'Orleans ordered his flag to be lowered and his servants put into mourning. After all, this was the only English sovereign most people could remember. The Mayor of Evesham sent the following telegram to the Home Secretary: 'In the name of the inhabitants of Evesham I desire to convey to the Royal family an expression of our profound sorrow and respectful sympathy in this sad hour. John S.Slater, Mayor.' The following year, the then Mayor, Councillor George Hughes, represented the town at the coronation of King Edward VII at Westminster Abbey.

A number of Evesham volunteers served in the Boer War, and their names are recorded on a plaque affixed to the town hall. There was much rejoicing in May 1900 when the town received news of the relief of Mafeking, and again after the conclusion of hostilities in 1902. Several events were organized in the town for the benefit of the returning soldiers. The same year saw the control of schools passing to the Worcestershire County Council and the ratepayers up in arms at having to contribute to the cost of education in the county.

'French' gardening was introduced to Evesham in 1906 principally by J.N.Harvey, whose nurseries were at the end of what is now Burford Road. The previous year, with a party of Evesham growers, he made a visit to France to study methods of horticulture under glass then used there with much success, and came back full of enthusiasm. He set aside an area of three quarters of an acre for his trials, and the land was laid out in a series of narrow beds with narrow walks between them. Upon these beds he placed glass frame lights or bell lights, and his enterprise was a great success, quickly followed by others; these methods are still used today, but mostly for plant growing. He was selling lettuces from 1 February onwards at 2s 6d to 3s 6d a crate, or approximately one penny each.

In 1910, after many years without, the members of Evesham town council appeared publicly with new official robes. The Mayor's was of crimson, deeply edged with fur, plus a cocked hat, the aldermen had crimson cloth gowns, but with less fur, and the councillors gowns of blue material and still less fur, plus cocked hats.

The election of 1910 of Mr Bolton Meredith Eyres as member of Parliament for South Worcestershire was the beginning of his exceptionally praiseworthy career as a parliamentarian and, during the war and after, as an officer in the Royal Navy. He became a commander and in 1931 First Lord of the Admiralty. He was High Steward of the borough of Evesham and first Viscount Monsell of Evesham. He represented the town until 1935, when he was succeeded by Sir Rupert de la Bere, who was to represent us for the following 20 years. He became Lord Mayor of London and was admitted an Honorary Freeman of the Borough of Evesham in 1953.

The new church of St Mary and St Egwin in High Street was opened in 1912 by the Archbishop of Birmingham, Dr Isley. This replaced the old iron Catholic church removed from Avon Street in 1900.

There was great controversy in Evesham early in 1914 over the purchase of land in Bengeworth for building houses for the working classes. Some fierce exchanges took place in the council chamber and in the press between Alderman Geoffrey New and the town clerk and members of the council, Mr New alleging that the signing of a land-purchase contract by Alderman Hughes, without first consulting all members of the council in the normal democratic way, was contrary to the Municipal Corporations Act of 1882. The arguments went on for months, but the 1914 war intervened and nothing more seems to have been said about it. The Council completed the purchase and the land was developed soon after the war to become Deacle Place, the town's first council housing enterprise.

The coming of the 1914 war barely a dozen years after the Boer War found the nation involved in what was to be the greatest test to date of its economic and manpower resources, and Evesham as a food-producing area had a big part to play. Many of the young men of the town who volunteered to serve could, had they so chosen, have remained at home and continued working on the land through-out, or at least until quite late in the war. The first to leave were the local volunteers, 'D' company of the 8th Worcesters based at Evesham, who marched from the Drill Hall in Coronation Street to the railway station for their first camp on 5 August 1914. Abbey Manor was quickly turned into a military hospital, and throughout the war, with a Red Cross detachment under the command of Mrs F. Haynes Rudge, hundreds of wounded soldiers were cared for there, many of them in later years returning to recall the kindness they received there and from the people of Evesham.

The Worcestershire War Agricultural Committee was set up in 1915, imposing numerous regulations and controls. but these affected Evesham and district much less than elsewhere, as the land was already under intensive cultivation, though some luxury crops were discontinued in favour of basic essentials. The gardeners again saw a time of considerable prosperity, and appeals in the town organized by the war savings committee raised large sums for War Loan Week, Tank Week, War Weapons Week. Evesham, apart from the constant unhappy reports of local casualties, suffered less than many communities, the only specifically local hardships being the conscription of some landworkers. The town's main war memorial in the Abbey Park to over 200 young men who died between 1914 and 1918 is considered to be one of the finest in Great Britain, and was unveiled on 7 August 1921 by the Earl of Coventry.

The years following the 1914-18 war saw a revival of interest in boating, sport, fishing, theatricals, and other leisure activities. By 1920 the Evesham Rowing Club had returned to full strength and their premier crew swept the board wherever they went and remained unbeaten throughout the season, carrying off 13 major trophies at various regattas.

It is hard to say when Evesham first had a football team as the game has been played in various forms for 1,000 or more years, but there has been a team in Evesham for as long as anyone can remember. Evesham Town F.C. had its ups and downs like all other clubs, but the season 1922/3 was to be their best ever. Not only were 'The Robins', as they were called, top of the Worcester league, but they also succeeded in making their mark in the world of sport by reaching the final of the English amateur football cup competition. They met the London Caledonians on 31 April 1923 at the Crystal Palace, and were unlucky to lose after extra time by two goals to one in a closely fought match.

Evesham also did well at cricket between the wars, producing some outstanding players. Their best year was probably 1934, when the first eleven were unbeaten and set up a number of club records, including a first-wicket unbroken stand of 249 between Sam

Johns and E.Grant Righton, three successive centuries by Sam Johns, and a fine match at Barnt Green for Wally Pritchard, who made 112 runs and took five wickets to bring his total to 32. Grant Righton was selected on three occasions for the county team.

The 1920s saw the start of a distinguished career in the world of music of one of Evesham's best known men, Victor Newbury, whose fine baritone voice brought so much pleasure to so many in the years which were to follow. In 1929 he took part in five musical festivals and won a first prize in each. His first gramophone record was made in 1930 and the first of his many broadcasts was in 1932, the fees being £5 5s 0d and £2 2s 0d respectively! In 1932 he toured with the famous Mark Hambourg, and by so doing greatly enhanced his reputation. Another Evesham singer, Miss Edith Ingram (later Mrs Edith Ingram Lewis), also had the honour of appearing with Mark Hambourg, and her fine voice has since brought much pleasure to audiences in Evesham and elsewhere. Vic Newbury's war-time broadcasts on the forces programmes, with the Midland Light Orchestra and others, were heard all over the world and brought many a serving man and girl from Evesham a breath of home. His local concert party, the Vale Singers, was in popular demand all over the midlands and beyond for something like a quarter of a century. One will never forget the comedians Ted Hall and Percy Sanger, pianist Billy Morton, and singers George Harrison and Eric Malin. Let us remember too the successes of various members of the musical Capaldi family of Evesham, particularly the skills of accordionists Carmino and Nicholas Capaldi, who distinguished themselves on the music hall stage as the Capaldi Brothers and the later husband and wife act of Marie and Nick.

1926 saw the opening of the corporation swimming baths on The Common, which were to serve the town for half a century. The following year saw the town's principal streets first lit by electricity.

The Abbey Bridge and viaduct, about half a mile downstream from the Workman Bridge, was erected in 1928 at a cost of over £40,000, and was opened by the then Minister of Transport, the Right Hon Wilfred Ashley. This was to be the answer to Evesham's traffic problems, and perhaps it was for a few years. This was followed by the incorporation of the parish of Great and Little Hampton into the borough.

The great depression of the 1930s, with the massive dole queues, so familiar in our larger towns and cities, did not have so great an effect upon Evesham, whose basic market gardening industry was supplemented by such enterprises as Willmott's Ltd, the spectacle case makers, Collins Bros., the pork pie, sausage, and meat processors, T.W.Beach & Sons, the jam manufacturers, and Smedley's, the fruit and vegetable canners, all large undertakings providing employment for men and women. By 1935 over 500 houses had been built for the council, a considerable post-war achievement for a small town.

By 1938 the fear of war was once again upon us and local authorities were busying themselves making preparations to protect the civilian population. When war came, with a nucleus of experienced First World War and ex-regular officers and men, Evesham formed its own unit of Local Defence Volunteers, later the Home Guard. Men and women joined the local A.R.P., and our young men and women again departed for active service. We soon saw an influx of land girls, evacuees, and wealthy fugitives from the big cities buying up empty houses. The B.B.C.'s establishment at Wood Norton was already on a war footing by the outbreak of war. The influx of actors, announcers, musicians, technicians, and foreign news monitors was quite traumatic. These people were known as the 'Guinea Pigs' (a reference to the billetting fee), and were popular, largely for the trade they brought shopkeepers, but the record of Evesham in the war years and after is another story.

George Ward, aged 26, on return from Boer War.

BOROUGH of EVESHAM

WORKMAN PLEASURE GROUNDS.

The Custodian of these Grounds has instructions to refuse admission to or permission to stay on the Grounds to Vagrants or persons conducting themselves in any way in a disorderly manner.

DATED this 3rd day of JULY, 1905.

By Order.

THOS. A. COX,
Town Clerk.

W. & H. SMITH LTD., The Journal Press, Evesham.

ABOVE: Leicester Gables and old Catholic church and schools; BELOW: notice re Workman pleasure grounds 1905.

ABOVE: Floods in Waterside 1900; BELOW: coronation dinner on Merstow Green 1902, and INSET: medal struck on the occasion of the coronation of King Edward VII and Queen Alexandra.

*ABOVE: Foundation stone-laying at new Wesleyan
Methodist church, 1906. BELOW: Procession to
opening of new Wesleyan Methodist church, 1907.*

LEFT: Opening ceremony at new Wesleyan Methodist church, 1907; RIGHT: B.M.Eyres-Monsell, MP - 1912; BELOW:opening of Swiss fete at Abbey Manor, 1909.

ABOVE: Market Place early in the century; BELOW:
group at Old English fair 1909.

By Appointment to H.R.H. the Duc d'Orleans.

7. VINE STREET. EVESHAM.   Mar: 25.   1911

Mr. West.   *Northwick Hotel*

Dr. to H. GOODALL,

CARRIAGE BUILDER,

SHOEING & GENERAL SMITH.

SPECIAL ATTENTION GIVEN TO BUILDERS' IRONWORK.

RUBBER TYRES, REPAIRS, REPAINTING, and TRIMMING.

Manufacturer of
CARRIAGES, · ·
TRAPS, VANS,
DRAYS and · · ·
BUSINESS CARTS
of Every Description.

CARRIAGE, CART
and DRAY LAMPS,
Etc.

WATERPROOF
COVERS and
OILSHEETS
At Lowest Prices.

ABOVE: H. Goodall's billhead, 1911; BELOW:
D.W.Knott and his sidecar outfit 1913, and
INSET: souvenir of Conservative fete at Abbey
Manor, 1912.

LEFT: Italian wedding at Evesham, 24 February 1908, of Joanna and Raphael Capaldi; ABOVE CENTRE: Evesham public library and reading room, c1907; and BELOW: Mayor and corporation 'send off' the local volunteers, 1914. ABOVE RIGHT: Men of the 8th Worcestershire at Malden, Essex, in 1914. CENTRE: In the trenches at Plugs Street. CENTRE BELOW: Belgian refugees in Market Place, c 1915; BELOW: Mrs Haynes-Rudge and Red Cross detachment at Abbey Manor hospital. Front row: Will Spiers, Mrs Haynes-Rudge, Noel Peal and F.J. Masters.

ABOVE: Nursing staff at Abbey Manor hospital, 1916. CENTRE: Invalid chairs and helpers at Vicarage garden, April 1916; BELOW: Evesham's Peace medal, 1919.

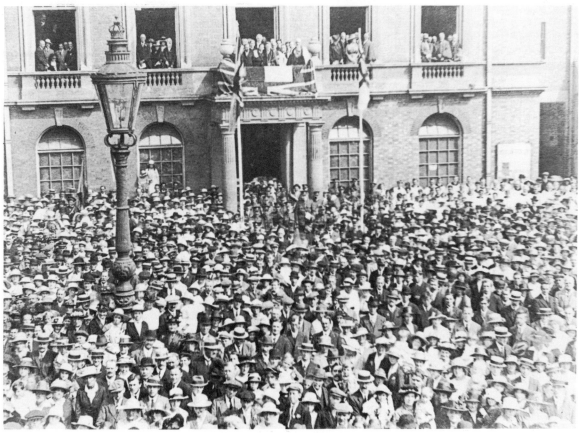

ABOVE: Meat queue in High Street 1918.
BELOW: Peace celebrations in Market Place 1919.

ABOVE: Peace celebrations at Merstow Green,
1919. BELOW: Unveiling Evesham's war memorial
in Abbey Park, 7 August 1921. INSET: The bronze
'Tommy' - part of Evesham's war memorial.

ABOVE: Evesham's champion crew, 1920; LEFT:
Evesham Town Football Club's supporters badge;
and RIGHT: 'The Robins', 1923.

ABOVE: Evesham's unbeaten cricket eleven, 1934.
Standing L.to R.: F.Pritchard (Umpire),
W.G.Pritchard, L.V.Newbury, J.W.Holmes,
K.W.S.Burnside, S.H.Johns, S.Bean. Seated: J.Beck
R.W.Beach, R.Randall (Captain), G.Bancks, N.H.Price
(E.G.Righton, Jnr, absent), G.Sharp (scorer);
BELOW: lady swimmers at Swimming Club in the
1930s.

ABOVE: Bell cloches - now very scarce. BELOW:
Forcing frames at Harveys French gardens.

*ABOVE: Tom Thumb cloches; BELOW: Fred Haines
with horse and dray.*

ABOVE: Henry Masters' premises on Benge Hill,
'F.J.Masters in cart in foreground); BELOW: outing
from The Jolly Gardeners in Bewdley Street.

*ABOVE: Early planting machine at Burlinghams,
1932. Left to right: Miss Taylor, Miss Watkins,
Mr. Dyde, Mr. Winnett, G.K. Bell and
R.G. Burlingham. BELOW: Char-a-banc leaving
Waterside.*

ABOVE: Yes, they are real asparagus heads!
BELOW: Percy Byrd driving his firm's new Seldon
30 cwt lorry supplied by Goodalls, 1920.

ABOVE: Lou Cockerton driving Henry Masters'
new Seldon lorry supplied by Goodalls, 1920.
BELOW: G.Ward & Sons' fleet of mobile shops
when operating from Kings Road, c 1925.

ABOVE: Clem Ward and vanman in High Street,
c 1925. BELOW: L.L.Farrington's garage in
Avon Street in the 1920s.

ABOVE: Goodalls' High Street garage, c 1930
BELOW: Interior of Goodalls garage, 1924.

*ABOVE: This early Morris of Mr. Pannell was a
familiar sight in Evesham in the 1920s and 1930s.
and BELOW: Evesham 'Wednesday' footballers,
c 1905.*

ABOVE: Mains electricity comes to Evesham 1927;
LEFT: Clem, George and Harry Ward, 1910, and
RIGHT: Evesham Salvation Army lassies, 1917;
BELOW: Salvation Army brass band (Evesham
Corps).

*ABOVE: Group at Bengeworth church 1918;
INSET: the new Catholic church and East Terrace,
High Street. BELOW: High Street scene, c 1925.*

*ABOVE: Rev J. Walker, when Vicar of Evesham,
with choristers. BELOW: Bengeworth school play,
c 1916, 'The Roman Invasion'.*

107

ABOVE Miss Clark's school at Almswood, c 1914;
BELOW Miss Morris's preparatory school for boys,
Bridge Street, c 1909.

ABOVE: Bengeworth school children, 1927;
BELOW: Wesleyan Mission Band, c 1900.

ABOVE: Frank Hampton's school attendance medal
1906-7. BELOW: Alcock family. Left to right:
Charles Hubert, Leslie Frank, Douglas Harold,
Frank Hubert and Frank Edwin.

ABOVE: Evesham Civil & Military Band, c 1919
BELOW: Church Lads' Brigade Band, 1916.

ABOVE: Ox soon to be slaughtered for the coronation ox roast 1902, and BELOW: tableaux at Evesham World Fair

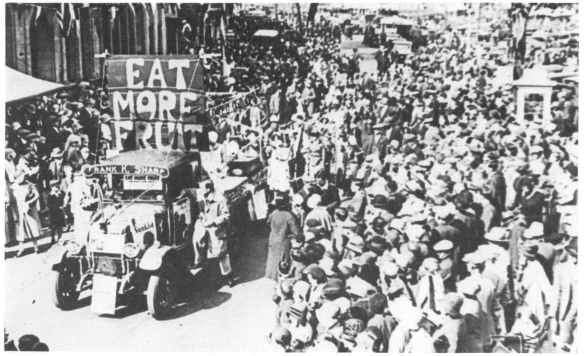

ABOVE: Hospital Gala ox roast, 1933; CENTRE:
hospital gala badges; BELOW: gala procession, 1931.

*ABOVE: Frank Malins' boathouse and tea-rooms
near Abbey Bridge, c 1930. BELOW: Disastrous
fire in the High Street, 1933.*

ABOVE: Evesham fire engine and crew, c 1930.
Left to right: Frank Clarke, Fred Halford, Harry
Lambert, Bert Emms, Lou Arthers, Jack Caldicutt
(driver). In front: Harry Rodway (Chief) and
Tom Emms (second man). BELOW: The last of
the poplars in Coopers Lane, 1903.

*ABOVE: The Northwick Arms, Waterside prior
to alterations. BELOW: High Street, 1911. The
large house in the centre was demolished to make
way for the Scala theatre (now Clifton cinema).*

*ABOVE: High Street, c 1928; LEFT: London House
and part of former Kings Head Hotel, c 1926;
RIGHT: G.H. Smith's shop in High Street, 1927.
Evesham's first telephone exchange was at these
premises.*

ABOVE: View of Workman Bridge and Wesleyan
chapel from window of non-existent hotel, and
BELOW: coming of age of Mr John E. Rudge, 1924.
Helpers at the children's party.

ABOVE: Lower Bridge Street, c 1923; BELOW:
Vine Street in the 1920s.

*ABOVE: Morris Bros., on site of former White
Hart Inn, Bridge Street, and BELOW: Abbey Bridge
in course of erection, 1928.*

ABOVE: Saturday in the Market Place, c 1925.
BELOW: Oat Street looking towards High Street.

LEFT ABOVE: Oat Street looking towards
Corners; CENTRE: Bewdley Street looking to
Clarks Hill, and BELOW: Bewdley Street lo
towards High Street. CENTRE ABOVE: High
in the mid 1930s - note Belisha crossing and

Scala theatre, and BELOW: Burlinghams' yard,
1934. RIGHT ABOVE: News from the Scala theatre,
CENTRE: special event at The Scala theatre 1932,
and BELOW: The Booth Hall (Round House) c 1928.

123

ABOVE: The Avon north of the Workman Bridge, c 1930; LEFT: Marie and Nick Capaldi, 1933; RIGHT: The Abbey Rythmic Dance Band, 1930s. Left to right: Grev Smith, Harry Jones, Doug Alcock, -Stott, Billy Morton. BELOW: The Avon Orchestra, 1930s. Back left to right: Percy Sanger, Cyril Hallam, Bill Field. Front left to right: Harry Jones, Arnold Salisbury, Frank Alcock, Billy Morton.

ABOVE: Doug Alcock's Dance Band, c 1935.
Left to right: Gordon Cox, Alf Grinnell, Doug
Alcock, Maurice Savory, Doug Dean, Frank Mace,
Grev Smith, 'Pinky' Green and Harry Jones; BELOW:
Evesham Town Council, 1935 (F.C.Hiden, Mayor).

ABOVE: Women's Land Army Group and BELOW & OPPOSITE: three companies of the Evesham Home Guard.

BIBLIOGRAPHY

Barnard, E.A.B. (ed)	Notes and queries. 3 vols (1911-14)
Barnard, E.A.B. (ed)	'Notes and queries'. Evesham Journal, 1906-16
Barnard, E.A.B. (ed)	'Old days in and around Evesham'. Evesham Journal, 1920-52
Beck, Mrs E.	When I was a little girl. Evesham 1952
Beck, Mrs E.	Shut up the Puppets. Evesham 1953
Cox, B.G.	Wood Norton. Evesham 1975
Cox, B.G.	The Book of Evesham (1977)
Gardiner, C.H.	Your village and mine (1944)
Gaut, R.C.	History of Worcestershire agriculture (1939)
May, G.	Descriptive history of the town of Evesham (1845)
New, E.H.	Evesham (Temple topographies) 1904
Noake, J.	Guide to Worcestershire (1868)
Noake, J.	Worcestershire nuggets (1889)
Noake, J.	Worcestershire relics (1877)
Rhodes, P.G.M.	Our Lady at Evesham (c. 1930)
Shawcross, J.P. and Bearnard, E.A.B.	Bengeworth (1927)
Smith, H.R.	Dark blue and white: the history of Evesham Rowing Club (1948)
Smith, H.R.	A Soldier's Diary (1940)
Smith, K.Gill	Story of an old meeting house 1737-1937 (1937)
Smith, W.	Evesham and the neighbourhood (Homeland Association's handbooks xxv, 1902 and 6 subsequent editions to 1937)
Turberville, T.C.	Worcestershire in the 19th century (1852)
Willis Bund, J.W. and Page, W. (eds)	Victoria history of the county of Worcester, ii (1906)

INDEX

Numbers in *italics* refer to illustrations

ACKNOWLEDGEMENTS

The authors would like to place on record the considerable help they have received from fellow members of the Vale of Evesham Historical Society, from the staff of the County Library service for their support, especially in providing facilities for intending subscribers, to Keith Barber and staff at Evesham public library, to A.M.Wherry and Miss Margaret Henderson of the county record office, C.W.T.Huddy for his great assistance over the years in recording material from which we have drawn; C.W.Clarke, editor of the *Evesham Journal*, for research facilities, to Christopher Alcock for his considerable help with the photographic work entailed, and to all those members of the public, too numerous to mention individually, who have, over the years, provided the old photographs and documents reproduced in this book, and for their recollections of Old Evesham on which we have drawn.

SUBSCRIBERS

Presentation copies

1 Evesham Town Council
2 Almonry Museum
3 Herefordshire and Worcestershire County Council
4 Evesham Branch Library
5 Pershore Branch Library

6 Benjamin G. Cox	63 Mrs S.B. Cook	122 Mrs E. Mary Cheer
7 D. Gordon Alcock	64 David J. Robbins	123 John Douglas Jelfs
8 Clive Birch	65 Richard & Josephine Smith	124 Philip Melvin Jelfs
9 Miss P. Williams	66 Harry Ward	125 Clifton W.T. Huddy
10 E.G. Anderson	67 Gilbert Smith	126 R.J. Laporta
11 Pauline Prew	68 R.J. Coombs	127 P.F. Stewart
12 Mr & Mrs D.J. Hall	69 Miss P.A. Collins	128 W.N. Redman
13 Mrs D.V. Reeve	70 Mrs C.M. Blackwell	129 A.H. Fryer
14 Janet Champan	71 Mrs L.A. Harris	130 Mrs Evelyn Hughes
15 Mrs J. Legelli	72 G.R. Dennick	131 L.C. Staite
16 B.J. Bluck	73 D.J. Porter	132 J.B. Heyes
17 Mr & Mrs H. Woolley	74 Mrs Mary Hitchman	133 J.L. Staite
18 M. Mumford	75 Mrs L.M. Ross	134 Mrs Albright
19 Miss G.I. Masters	76 Mr & Mrs R.A. Thould	135- R.G. Burlingham
20 Frederick & Sheila Taylor	77 Mrs S. Knight	137
21 Mrs M. Tarver	78 Mrs B. Mayes	138 W.R. Rogers
22 S.B. Emms	79 Peter J. Larner	139 J.H. Fryer
23 Alan & Jean Whitehouse	80 Graham A. Rodway	140 Walt & Doris Such
24	81 Ian W.M. Roper	141 Ron & Barbara Bostock
25 Henry W. King	82 Mrs W.F. Tomblin	142 Percy & Mona Taylor
26 Mrs F.A. Williams	83 K. Skidmore	143 Christopher Robin Alcock
27 Dr W.J. Barry	84 M. Hemming	144 Mr & Mrs K.A. Hawkard
28 B. Loxley	85 J.J. Guoite	145 C.C. Grove
29 J.I. Keen	86 Miss Betty Bayford	146 D.W. Hildred
30 H. Williams	87 Mrs Freda I. Durose	147 M.A. Martin
31 Mrs E. Nicholls	88 Mrs V. Newbury	148 M.A. & S.E. Print
32 Martin T. King	89 Miss B.M. Harris	149 K.D. Sinclair
33 Alison L. King	90 Miss W.E. Hawker	150 Verna & Edd Taylor
34 Stephen M. King	91 Michael Ellison	151 Kath & Fred Mayer
35 Brian E. Barry	92 Miss N.M. Hughes	152 A.G. Lowe
36 Peter Chard	93 W.C. Astley	153 J.E.L. Goodall
37 Mr & Mrs G.J. James	94 Mrs E.A. Price	154 E.S. Goodall
38 F. Taylor	95 J.T. Cox	155 Mrs Norah Gwendoline Alcock
39 Miss J.M. Tomlin	96 David C. Cox PhD FSA	156 Mrs Maud Wilkinson
40 Mrs J. Hancox	97 Peter J. Lippett	157 Mrs Dorothy Tarry
41 G.W. Haywood	98 Christopher Mancrief	158 Henry J.H. Saunders
42 Simon de Montfort Middle School	99 R.V. Smith	159 Miss Ivy Hampton
	100 R.A. Dyson	160 John Morris
44 Mrs D.M. Hale	101 Brian E. Keyte	161 Stephen Baldwin
43 Mrs A. Metzger	103 M.J. Smith	162 Mrs Ann Gisborne
45 B. Lambert	104 Miss J.E.A. Arthur	163 Mrs P. Baker
46 W.H.N. Saunders	105 I.S. Simmonds	164 B.J. Waite
47 Brian Last	106 Mr & Mrs M.L. Warren	165 P.R. Pitman
48 Stephen Pinchin	107 Mrs W. Parrott	166 Michael Alcock
49 Maurice E. Wadams	108 Mrs H. Webster	167 Mrs Josephine Mary Alcock
50 Lesley Faith Abbott	109 Janet Percival	168 R.A. Colwell
51 David & Trudi Hirons	110 Mr & Mrs C.J. Pilling	169 L. Dallard
52 Ronald Smith	111 J.H. Cook	170 P.W.L. Mitchell
53 G.R. Montagu	112 Mr & Mrs E.G. Cook	171 A.C. Wheeler
54 P.G. Francis	113 Kevin Paul Alcock	172 K.C. Skidmore
55 S.H. Vale	114 Mr & Mrs C.D. Barr	173 John A. Groom
56 P. Robbins	115 Dr L.M. Cox	174 Margaret Sharp
57 David F. Witts	116 Robert Shephard	175 W.E. Beckley
58 Miss B.M. Tate	117 Eric & June Boden	176 Sheila Grant
59	118 Grant & Marilyn Boden	177 George Lionel Cooper
60 Miss P. Williams	119 Maurice Lionel Carter	178 Mrs. M.H. Barnes
61 A.W. Watton	120 Neville & Glenys Cole	179 Rev & Mrs D.H. Martin
62 D.R. Barnes	121 Mr & Mrs A.D. Knott	180 Mrs M.E. Clutton

181 John R. Lewis
182 G. Hilton
183 Edward Philip de Franco
184 C.P. Barnard
185 Judith I. Todd
186 D.M. Kirby
187 G.W. Dawson
188 L.H. Young
189 R.H. Palmor
190 R. & D. Davies
191 Nancy M. Hughes
192- A.H. Edwards
195
196 M. Johns
197 Mrs V.E. Peart
198 F.G. Evans
199 Derek W. Wright
200 M.F. Page
201 M.G. Collins
202 F.N. Righton
203 N.P. Finlay
204 R.J. & M.T. Kyte
205 Miss P.M.S. Vincent
206 H.E. Brotheridge
207 Peter & Maureen Chew
208 E. Darke
209 T.S. Cox
210 Anthony J. Brazier
211 David H. Brazier
212
213 Mr & Mrs R.C.K. Thomson
214 S.J. Bragginton
215 Charles T. Burch
216 John E. Loudoun
217 E. Bradshaw
218 Mrs P.A. Richardson
219 C.M. Barry
220 R.W. Kyte
221 Joan Clarke
222 Prince Henrys High School
223 Evesham High School
224 Miss A.H. Gibb
225 R.K. Swift
226
227 Kenneth Gill-Smith

228 T. Bruce Bayley
229 Carol J. Yates
230 Miss S.C. Ashfield
213 R.A. Spragg
232 Mr & Mrs Peter Silverton
233 Evesham College of Further Education
234 George Aldrich
235 W.B. Albright
236 Dr J.M. Wilson
237
238 Ian M. Andrews
239 H.G. Parry
240
241 H.C. Martin
242 Mrs M. Watson
243 Donald Barnard
244 Evesham Town Council
245 Miss June Abbotts
246- John Robert Turner
248
249 A.J. de N. Rudge
250
251 M.J. Moore
252
253 W. Wahle
254 Thomas L. Cox
255 Mrs J. Shackleton
256 H.V. Cooke
257 C.A. Message
258 E.J. Lofthouse
259 Robert John Curtis
260 M.J. Hancock
261 Mr & Mrs D. Ellis
262 J. Williams
263 Mrs B. Haines
264 D.F. Brotherton
265 A.H. Penson
266 Peter and Michael Jones
267 F.E. Hampton
268 Enid Ballinger
269 N.F. Davies
270 Eric Edwin Poole
271 Iris Jordan

Remaining names unlisted.

272 Edgar R. Brotherton
273 Mrs N.E. Randall
274 Henry Asawin
275 Barry J. Hall
276 Michael Walters
277 M.V. Tittensor
278 Gordon W. Lauder
279 Julian Laurie-Beckett
280
281 Mrs D.M. Hodgkinson
282
283 A.V. Crowle
284 M.J. Franklin
285 M.T. Anderson
286 Mrs R.B. Powis
287 A.W. Watton
288 Mrs B.A. Sampson
289 Zoe Elizabeth Reeve
290 Mr & Mrs T. Pitcher
291 G.W.J. Kite
292 Mr & Mrs P.J. Newman
293 George R. Davie
294 J.J. & M.M. Featherstone
295 Mrs D.M. Spiers
296 Mrs J. Thompson
297 Alexander Marshall
298 Mrs R.W. Chatfield
299
300 K.C. Lane
301 Malcolm T. Barlow
302 Mrs J. Turvey
303 David Read
304 Malcolm Read
305 Victoria & Albert Museum
306 Joan & Tony Lammiman
307- Hereford & Worcester County
338 Library
339 Albert Grove
340 Ian R. Stanton
341 J.E. Grey
342 Ernest E. Butler
343 Mr & Mrs David Eaves
344 Brian J. Barber
345 Mrs Irene E. Blacktin

END PAPERS: FRONT: *Evesham estate map c 1840 with line of proposed*
railway added later.

BACK:
ABOVE: *Old Evesham bridge from Waterside 1854*
by E.H.New. From an original painting
by T.Colson.
BELOW: *Old Evesham bridge from Avon Bank*
1854 by E.H.New. From an original paint-
ing by T.Colson.